Théodore M. R. Bussiere

The Conversion of Marie-Alphonse Ratisbonne

Théodore M. R. Bussiere

The Conversion of Marie-Alphonse Ratisbonne

ISBN/EAN: 9783337300227

Printed in Europe, USA, Canada, Australia, Japan

Cover: Foto ©Lupo / pixelio.de

More available books at **www.hansebooks.com**

THE CONVERSION OF MARIE-ALPHONSE RATISBONNE:

ORIGINAL NARRATIVE OF

BARON THÉODORE DE BUSSIÉRES;

FOLLOWED BY A LETTER FROM MR. RATISBONNE TO REV. MR. DUFRICHE-DESGENETTES CURÉ OF NOTRE-DAME DES VICTORIES AT PARIS.

EDITED BY THE REV. W. LOCKHART,
OF THE ORDER OF CHARITY.

NEW YORK:
P. J. KENEDY,
PUBLISHER TO THE HOLY APOSTOLIC SEE,
EXCELSIOR CATHOLIC PUBLISHING HOUSE,
3 AND 5 BARCLAY STREET.
1897.

WHILE I affirm that all the facts contained in this narrative are related with rigorous exactness, and with the sincerest truth, I declare, in compliance with the decree of Urban VIII. that I believe them as facts resting simply on human testimony, and on motives of human reason alone.

THE BARON DE BUSSIÈRES.

Rome, 17*th February*, 1842.

PREFACE.

WE have given in this volume a literal translation of the original accounts of the conversion of M. Alphonse Ratisbonne. The attempt to construct an independent narrative would be presumptuous in itself, and would lose the simple force and freshness of these genuine documents. Those who know the scrupulous and almost suspicious care with which the pretensions of any alleged miracle are tested at Rome, will feel the value of the decree of the Cardinal-Vicar which is prefixed. Baron de Bussières prefaced his first edition with a declaration, that he claimed for his narrative only that measure of assent which may be granted to any ordinary statement, resting on human evidence alone; this decree has raised the conversion of Mr. Ratisbonne to the position of an accredited miracle.

It is both sad and strange to observe the air of superb disdain with which miracles such as this are set aside, even by those who seem least removed from the Church, and who profess to accept the miracles of Holy Scripture on their own evidence, and to be familiar with the laws of moral reasoning.

And yet, surely, those who reject this statement as an imposture or a delusion, should feel bound to show wherein it lacks the criteria of a true miracle. We may assume that they will be unwilling to affirm that the power of working miracles was restrained within the limits of the apostolic age; they know that this hypothesis is fatal to historical Christianity, and belies the promise of its inspired records. Nor will they say that a miracle is so improbable a thing in the kingdom of God that no amount of testimony can render it credible; they know well, that on this view, they could hardly rescue the miracles of the Gospels from the hands of unbelievers.

They must rest their rejection on one of these grounds: they either regard the evidence for this particular miracle as insufficient or untrustworthy; or they shrink from doctrines and practices which seem to them imbedded in it, or presupposed by it.

Yet they have learnt from a great authority amongst themselves,* that objections to any revelation from God, as distinguished from objections to its evidence, are frivolous. It is not competent to them to set aside credible testimony to a miracle, simply because that miracle carries with it theologi-

* *Butler's Analogy*, Part II. ch. iii.

cal consequences which they deem at variance with the general scheme of religion. Nor would they thus reserve any right to blame the Jews for rejecting our Lord's miracles. The only question which they can logically entertain is the evidence for this particular miracle—the apparition of the Blessed Virgin to Alphonse Ratisbonne in the church of St. Andrea at Rome.

And if we weigh the character of the witness and his competency; the improbability of his being deceived or wishing to deceive; the simple fact of the entire change wrought upon him in a moment, in the conversion of his heart and the illumination of his mind; the consequences of his testimony to himself; and then, the many years which have tested his sincerity and his stability;— if we weigh all these circumstances, we may ask whether it is possible to decline to receive his testimony on any grounds which would not excuse the Jews that dwelt at Damascus for refusing to credit the conversion of Saul of Tarsus, and Festus for deeming him mad. We repeat, that those who feel that there is no antecedent improbability in the occurrence of miracles, that the later miracles cannot be discredited on *à priori* grounds without shaking the credit of those of the Gospels, are bound to justify their rejection of this miracle by impeaching its evidence. This is the only issue which a Christian can properly raise; and that testimony cannot be trivial or indifferent which the Church has stamped with the seal of its acceptance.

But here we would invite attention to some weighty and suggestive remarks of Cardinal Wiseman, in his review of a pamphlet entitled *A Voice from Rome.**

"In proof that the Blessed Virgin is worshipped as the Mother of mercies, temporal and spiritual, the author before us appeals to the Baron de Bussières' account of M. Ratisbonne's conversion from Judaism, 'which he distinctly attributes to the immediate operation of the Virgin Mary; for he relates, that it was effected by her actual appearance to him.' Now, what is meant to be granted, and what is meant to be doubted here, we do not know. We suppose that no one doubts that M. Ratisbonne, from a Jew, did become a Catholic, and has become a religious; having abandoned home and friends, and given up a long-cherished alliance. Any one might as well deny that Sir R. Peel is prime minister. That he went into the church of St. Andrew a Jew, and came out a Christian, is attested upon evidence as certain as any fact can well be—that of trustworthy and honest men, who saw him and spoke with him before and after. For the change something must account. That it was a *true* conversion from Judaism to Christianity, with great temporal sacrifices, is clear; and such a conversion must have been the work of divine grace. How communicated is the question. The only witness can be the convert. He tells us that it was through an apparition of the Mother of God, who instructed him in the mysteries of our holy religion. Are we to believe that a person is chosen by the Divine Goodness for an object of a most

* *Dublin Review*, Dec. 1843. Cardinal Wiseman's Essays, vol. i. 550

singular act of grace, at the moment that he devises and tells an abominable falsehood, to rob Him of the glory of it, and give it to another, by feigning a vision of the Blessed Virgin? What does the author of the *Voice* mean to throw doubt on? on the apparition, as for such a purpose impossible? or on the consequences drawn from it? Surely not on the latter; for if the vision was true, it was right to consider the blessed Mother of God, not as the *source*, but as the *channel*, of a great 'spiritual mercy.'

"If he wish to insinuate that it would be derogatory to God's honour, or incompatible with His revealed doctrines, to believe such a mode of communicating grace and religious instruction possible, and consequently, that the whole must be a figment or a delusion, we will, in answer, relate another similar story, in which not a Jew, but a bishop, was the party; and we will premise that we have it on the best authority.

"The person to whom we allude was a young man of singular piety and virtue. Left young an orphan, he devoted his youth to study in a celebrated university. There his assiduity in learning was surpassed only by the purity and innocence of his life, which stood the test of severe trials, and escaped the snares laid for him by profligate companions, jealous of his virtue. Having made himself master of all profane learning, he entered on a course of sacred studies, under the most celebrated professor of the day, and soon made considerable progress. He was, however, while yet young, put into orders, and even named bishop, before he considered himself well enough grounded in theological knowledge; though probably his humility led him to exaggerate his deficiencies. He found himself quite unequal to the task of preaching the Divine Word; and on the eve of his first undertaking this duty, he lay sleepless on his bed, in agitation and anxiety. Suddenly he saw before him a venerable figure of an old man, whose countenance, attitude, and garb, bespoke great dignity, but who, at the same time, appeared most gracious and affable. Terrified at this appearance, he leaped from his couch, and respectfully asked who he was, and for what purpose he had come. The old man replied, in a gentle voice, that he had come to calm his doubts and solve his difficulties. This declaration soothed his fears, and made him look towards his visitor with a mixture of joy and awe; when he perceived, that by steadily pointing with his hand towards the other side of the apartment, he seemed to wish to turn his attention in that direction. Thither he consequently turned his eyes, and there he beheld a lady of peerless majesty, and of more than human beauty, so resplendent that his eyes could not bear the brightness of the vision, but he must needs bend them and his countenance down, in reverential awe. Thus he listened to the conversation of these two heavenly beings, which fully instructed him on the subjects whereon he felt anxious, and at the same time informed him who his gracious visitors were. For the lady, addressing the other by the name of the Evangelist John, requested him to instruct the youth in the mystery of heavenly piety; and he replied, 'that he was ready to do even this, to please the Mother of his Lord, seeing that she desired it.' And accordingly he did so.

"Such is our counterpart to the narrative objected to by our author, respecting M. Ratisbonne's conversion. Now, before giving the name of our authority for this wonderful history, or of the person to whom it refers, we will only beg our reader, if not sufficiently versed in ecclesiastical biography, at once to answer both points, to say to what Church or religion he considers either the writer or the subject of this anecdote belongs. Could he believe us, if we told him that it happened to Bishop Ken, or Bishop Wilson, or Archbishop Laud; or that we had transcribed it, as gravely told by some Anglican clergyman in a life of any of them? We are sure he would not. The idea of a Protestant Bishop learning his faith from a vision of the Blessed Virgin, would be deemed repugnant to every principle and every feeling of the religion. But were we to tell the reader that the bishop spoken of was St. Alphonsus Liguori, or even St. Charles, and the narrator an Italian monk or priest, he would at once allow, that such an account, from such a pen, concerning such a person, was perfectly consistent with the principles of both; and though, if a Protestant, he might declare that he did not believe the story, he would acknowledge that it did not surprise him to find it in such a place. It must, then, be a Catholic, and not a Protestant, who thought or said he saw such a vision; and it must be a Catholic, and not a Protestant, who has recorded it, as believing it. And so it was. The bishop who thus learnt his faith was St. Gregory Thaumaturgus, only little more than two hundred years after Christ; and 'the recorder of the vision is the brother of the great St. Basil, St. Gregory, Bishop of Nyssa. This would have been a nice anecdote for our ancient note-taker upon the doctrines of Catholics."

The real reason why miracles such as this are rejected with scorn, or passed by with indifference, is not their antecedent improbability nor the inadequacy of their evidence; it is that they imply and render sensible the position and power of the blessed Mother of God. The Protestant cannot endure that glad and graceful vision of the Mother of Divine Grace—*radios evibrans misericordiæ suæ*— as Catholic piety delights to image her. It is an offence to him. It is something so intolerable to him, that, in his antipathy, he forgets all canons of moral reasoning; his conceptions and definitions become confused, and he allows this consoling vision to neutralise the positive evidence, that the Church which discloses it is alone of God.

And yet waving in thought what we can never forget in fact, that clear voice of the Church which is the Catholic's warrant of faith, why should it be thought a thing so violently incredible that the Mother of God should occupy the position, and exercise the powers, ascribed to her by the Church ?' Surely there can be no natural and necessary improbability in that which East and West combine to affirm. Except in the fancies of a modern and very small section of the nominally Christian world, there has never been any consciousness of an incompatibility between our assigned office and the Gospel. Her glories and prerogatives, as Mother of Christians and a special channel of grace, have not shocked the wisest and the holiest sons of the Church.

Nor can those who rightly ascribe so tremendous an influence to Eve over the destinies of our race, rightfully shrink from the range of power attributed by the Church to the advocate and counterpart of Eve. It cannot, surely, be a gratuitous fancy to see in the effects of the unbelief and disobedience of the mother of all living, in the order of nature, a hint and a measure, though not a limit, of the efficacy of the faith and obedience of the mother of all living, in the order of grace.

But let us observe here, that the miraculous

element in the conversion narrated in this volume is simply the apparition of the blessed Mother of God, and not her intercessory power. The Catholic regards that power as a supernatural fact, a law of the spiritual kingdom, one of *the powers of the world to come.* He needs no miracle to teach him that. No number or splendour of miracles could increase his faith in that. They would be but verifications to sense of what he knows already, absolutely and infallibly, by the teaching of the Church; what he sees already, by the deep intuition of faith. Such a miracle as this might excite his faith, but could not be its ground or warrant. He sees the office and the prerogatives of the Blessed Virgin involved in the fact of the Incarnation. *Mary, of whom was born Jesus*—he needs no more. Mary, Mother of God; Mary, bequeathed to us as our mother from the Cross: the Divine Maternity includes and implies all. Her glories and her mighty powers are only its natural consequences, and its fitting adornment.

Is he reminded of the absence of express command to seek her intercession? He feels that he has the command of that same Spirit by whose inspiration Scripture was written. For the Church can ever say, *it hath thus seemed good to the Holy Ghost and to us.* He would remind the objector, that the relation in which the Mother of God stands to us being known, the duty of religious regard to her, on Bishop Butler's principles, arises out of that relation itself, and is an obligation of reason, binding as soon as that relation is known. It is our duty as well as our privilege to seek the intercession of those who have power with God; and he would call on the objector to produce some prohibition of so natural an exercise of that privilege. And, indeed, Catholics feel that this objection does strike at intercessory prayer in general. There is, we know, an intercession, vast and mighty, which rests upon and carries out, if we may so speak, the great mediation of the Word made flesh; and that mediation is a legitimate object of desire, and consequently of petition, to every Christian man. It is for the objector to produce a command in limitation of this our right, in the covenant of grace.

But then, to invoke the Blessed Mother, to imagine that she can hear our cry and turn on us her pitying eyes—it is this which is deemed so absurd as to need no refutation. As if the charge of absurdity did not recoil on those who, with gross conceptions, impose on the world unseen the laws of space and time and the like, which rule this world that is seen; who dare to limit the range of the perceptions of the blessed by the laws of man's bodily senses, senses which are but the spirit's points of contact with the material world. Surely, it is both shallow and unscientific to reason from the senses of *this body of our lowness*, to the powers and perceptions of the saints who reign with Christ. Be it so, that we know not precisely how the Saints hear our invocations. It is enough, to turn the force of this objection drawn from our ignorance, to say that we can conceive many ways in which they may know the desires of our hearts. It is quite enough for the Catholic to say: what if

> A sea before
> The throne is spread; its pure still glass
> Pictures all earth-scenes as they pass.
> We, on its shore,
> Share, in the bosom of our rest,
> God's knowledge, and are blest.

Still there is a jealousy, honourable in its motive, most unwise in its conclusions, that our recourse to the Blessed Mother of Christians does in some way interfere with the simplicity of our trust in Jesus. It is impossible for those who are without, to understand the practical and ever-present safeguards of the Catholic from all error, from all excess. They cannot know, for instance, the effect of the Mass in regulating all his language and thoughts; nor how impossible it is that this perception of the greatness of the powers which God does communicate to the creature, should lessen the greatness, or dim the glory of those which are incommunicable. Surely it should suffice to affirm that the sole Mediatorship of the Incarnate Son of God is the very condition of all Catholic theology and practice. Like the weakness of man and the might of grace, it is a law of the spiritual order, every where felt, every where presupposed, every where taken for granted, underlying every statement, pointing every prayer. It is not so much a part of the Gospel, as the Gospel itself. But the intercession of the Blessed Virgin and of the Saints cannot be so stated as to clash with this oneness of mediation. They cannot ask otherwise than in accordance with His will, nor apart from His great pleading. It is upon that golden altar, which is before the throne of God, that the prayers of all saints are offered, in St. John's vision. Now this is ever present to the Catholic. However largely he may ask of our Blessed Mother—and he does ask largely —the principle of his asking and the law of its interpretation are, *Tu da, per precata dulcisona*— by thy sweet prevailing prayer. However wide and, to human notions unlimited, the range of power he ascribes to the Mother of God, it abides still an *omnipotentia supplex*, as St. Bernard beautifully says. It cannot be otherwise to him. He is never even tempted to confound the creatures with the Creator, to mistake the streams for the source.

But, indeed, it is not the illumination of the mind that is needed to bring back the strayed sheep to the fold; it is the attraction of the heart and the bending of the will, and this is the work of God alone. Would those who doubt and object but meditate awhile on the solitary prerogative of Mary, on her proximity to the flesh of Jesus, and on the intensity of the mutual love that must bind together that Son and that Mother; would they but try to look at her revealed position from the Church's point of view, with all those limitations and checks and safeguards of which they can form no notion; would they do this, not with the hard cold gaze of the intellect, but with a loving docile heart; the objections which now hang like clouds before their soul's eye would melt away of themselves and leave no trace. To such a one we would say, in all affection, if you must reason ere you believe, remember the laws which control all moral reasoning; remember that no number of even irreducible objections are of weight against that which rests upon direct and positive evidence; remember that though this evidence is " liable to objections, and may be run up into difficulties, it is not lost in these difficulties or destroyed by these objections;"* remember that those who, like St. Bernard, St. Anselm, St. Bonaventura, St. Alphonsus, have been most devout to Mary, have spoken of Jesus with the tongues of angels rather than of men; and pray—*ora fortiter et fideliter.* And as you gaze,

* *Butler's Analogy*, Part II chap. vi.

you will see how the Mother of Jesus is the mother of His mystical body likewise—*Mater membrorum Ejus*, as St. Augustine speaks. As you fathom the import of the words, *Behold the handmaid of the Lord*, you will come to feel that it is a mighty plea and an availing, to say, *Behold, O Lord, how that I am Thy servant, and the son of Thine handmaid;* and you will soon be enabled to continue the words of the psalm, *Thou hast broken my bonds asunder.*

We owe an apology to our Catholic readers for the length to which these remarks have extended. *You* can hardly grasp the reality of the difficulty which Protestants feel in the intercession of the Blessed Virgin and of the Saints. You can scarcely believe that men, believing the mystery of the Incarnation, can really confound things so accordant indeed, yet so distinct, as the affiance of a Christian in Christ, and his recourse to the prayers of all saints, without intellectual weakness or moral perversity. To you the miracle related here is, if I may so speak, quite natural and in keeping; wonderful indeed, but still what you are prepared to expect from the Mother of mercy.

To you all Scripture speaks of her, in type and figure, in prophecy and promise. To you the Incarnation is unintelligible apart from her, and doctrine heterodox or unmeaning which makes no mention of her. You know that as you have loved

Jesus more, you have felt for her whom He loved best on earth, whom He cannot but delight to honour in heaven—a truer, deeper, more loyal, and more trustful love; and that as your devotion to the Mother of God has gathered strength, you have known and loved Jesus with a less reserved and less reserving love. You know and feel that God has indeed done great things unto her; but it has never occurred to you that He has thereby dimmed the glory of His name. You have rather said with her—*et sanctum nomen Ejus.*

This narrative is of conversion, of Mary's tender pity towards those who know her not. How can we better express our thankfulness for this instance of her compassion than by praying for those to whom that very compassion is an offence and a hindrance? We know, by manifold experience—*we have heard with our ears, and our fathers have declared it to us*—the reality, the range, and the patience of that compassion. Let us pray for those who, from amidst their gathering gloom, are casting wistful, timid looks towards the one unwavering light, that God's grace may still lead them on, and gently clear their way through their thorny objections, until it

<blockquote>
brings them under Mary's smile
And Peter's royal feet.
</blockquote>

Decree verifying and accrediting the Miraculous Conversion of MARIE-ALPHONSE RATISBONNE.

In the name of God. Amen.

IN the year of our Lord and Saviour Jesus Christ one thousand eight hundred and forty-two, being the fifteenth of the Roman Indiction, and the twelfth year of the Pontificate of our Holy Father Pope Gregory XVI., and on the third day of June.

In the presence of the Very Eminent and Reverend Constantine Cardinal Patrizi, Vicar-General of our Holy Father the Pope, Ordinary Judge of the Roman Court . . . . appeared the Very Reverend Francis Anivitti, Proctor-Fiscal of the tribunal of the Vicariate, who had been specially deputed by the Very Eminent and Reverend the Cardinal-Vicar, to make inquiry and to examine witnesses in regard of the truth and reality of the wonderful conversion from Judaism to the Catholic Religion, granted, through the intercession of the Blessed Virgin Mary, to Alphonse Ratisbonne, a native of Strasburg, twenty-eight years of age, and now present in this city: the which Proctor declares that he applied himself to the inquiry intrust-

In Dei Nomine. Amen.

ANNO a salutiferâ D. N. J. C. Nativitate milles. octogentes. quadragesimo secundo, Indict. Rom. XV., Pontificatus autem sanctissimi D. N. PP. Gregorii XVI. ann. XII. die vero tertiâ Junii.

Coram Eminentissimo ac Reverendissimo Constantino Card. Patrizi, sanctissimi D. N. PP., in almâ urbe Vicario-Generali, Romanæque curiæ ejusque districtus Judice Ordinario . . . . . . comparuit Reverendissimus D. Franciscus Anivitti, Promotor Fiscalis tribunalis Vicariatus, ab eodem Eminentissimo ac Reverendissimo D. Card. Vicario specialiter delegatus, ad effectum inquirendi et examinandi testes super veritate et relevantiâ mirabilis conversionis ab Hebraismo ad Catholicam religionem, quam, intercedente B. V. Mariâ, obtinuit Alphonsus-Maria Ratisbonne, Strasburgensis, anno viginti octo, in urbe præsens; dixitque muneri sibi demandato, alacri libentique animo suscepto, quâ potuit sedulitate ac diligentiâ satisfacere studuisse,

ed to him with the utmost care and diligence, and with a ready and willing mind. He declares further, that he has submitted the witnesses, to the number of nine, to a formal examination, and that they all display a marvellous agreement in their account of the alleged fact, and of its consequences and results. Whereupon he declared that, in his judgment, nothing was wanting in the characteristics of a true miracle; but that, nevertheless, he referred the decision of the question to his Eminence, and besought him to issue a definitive decree, as it might seem to him expedient in the Lord, after a full examination of the acts and documents laid before him.

Whereupon the Very Eminent and Reverend Cardinal-Vicar, having received the report, and read the questions proposed to the witnesses, together with their answers; and after mature and careful consideration of the same, after having also taken the advice and judgment of theologians and other holy men, in the form required by the Council of Trent, Session 25, *de invocatione*, &c., pronounced and declared definitively, that he affirmed the reality and truth of the miracle wrought by God, at the intercession of the Blessed Virgin Mary, in

subjiciendo formali examini numero novem testes, qui, omnes ad fiscalia interrogatoria respondentes, ingenuâ enarratione, in iis quæ ad substantiam facti et mirabilis eventus extrema pertinent, mire concordant. Quamobrem sibi visum esse asseruit, nihil ad rationem veri miraculi ulterius posse desiderari. Rem tamen omnem definiendam remisit Eminentiæ suæ Reverendissimæ, quæ, visis et examinatis actis, examinibus et documentis, definitivum decretum prout in Domino expedire ei videbitur, interponere dignabitur.

Et tunc Eminentissimus ac Reverendissimus D. Card. in urbe Vicarius, auditâ relatione, viso processu, visis testium examinibus, juribus, ac documentis, iis sedulo matureque consideratis, consultationibus etiam requisitis theologorum aliorumque piorum virorum, juxta formam Concilii Tridentini, Sess. 25, de invocatione, veneratione, et reliquiis sanctorum, ac sacris imaginibus, dixit, pronuntiavit, et definitive declaravit. plene constare de vero insignique miraculo, a D. O. M. intercedente B. Mariâ Virgine, patrato, videlicet instantaneæ

the instantaneous and perfect conversion from Judaism of Alphonse Ratisbonne aforesaid. And, inasmuch as it is *honourable to confess and reveal the works of God*, his Eminence is pleased to permit that this narrative be printed and published, and held as authentic, for the glory of God, and for the increasing the devotion of all true Christians to the Blessed Virgin Mary.

Given at the palace of the aforesaid Very Eminent and Reverend Cardinal-Vicar and Ordinary Judge, on the day, month, and year aforesaid.

C. CARD. Vicar.
CAM. DIAMILLA, Notary,
JOSEPH, Chancellor.
TARNASSI, Secretary.

A true copy.

✠

Place of the seal.

perfectæque conversionis Alphonsi-Mariæ Ratisbonne ab Hebraismo. Et quoniam opera Dei relevare et confiteri honorificum est (Tob. xii. 7), ideo ad majorem Dei gloriam, et ad augendam devotionem Christi fidelium erga B. Virginem Mariam, benigne in Deo concessit, ut præfati insignis miraculi relatio publicis typis tradi, impressaque evulgari possit, et valeat.

Datum ex ædibus ejusdem Eminentissimi D. Cardinalis, urbis Vicarii et Judicis Ordinarii, die, mense et anno quibus supra.

C. CARDIN., Vicarius
CAM. DIAMILLA, Not. Deput.
JOSEPH, Can.
TARNASSI, Sec.

Concordat cum originali.

✠

Loco sigilli.

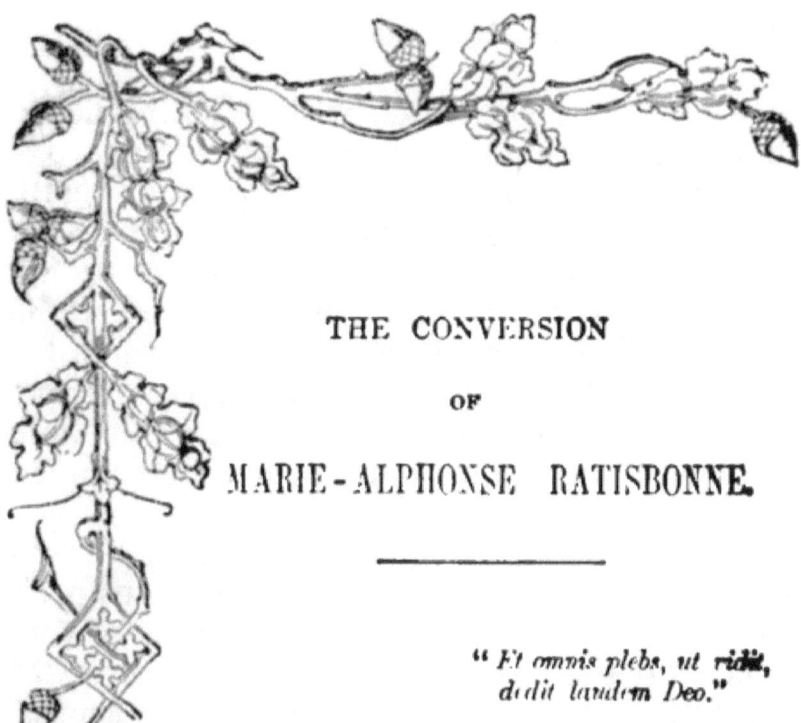

THE CONVERSION

OF

MARIE-ALPHONSE RATISBONNE.

"*Et omnis plebs, ut ridit, dedit laudem Deo.*"

He who made use of a little clay from the way-side to open to the light of heaven the eyes of him that had been born blind, permitted me to be the chief witness of an event of which human reason alone can render no adequate account. The fact I am about to relate is beyond dispute. I am to speak of what I saw with my own eyes—of what a multitude of competent and trustworthy witnesses confirm—a man, in full possession of all his senses and faculties, entered a church an obstinate Jew; and, by one of those swift flashes of grace which laid Saul prostrate at the gates of Damascus, he came forth, ten minutes afterwards, a Catholic in heart and in will.

Towards the close of the autumn of 1841,

a young man, connected with a distinguished family at Strasburg, arrived at Naples. He was on his way to the East, in quest of health and pleasure: yet it was not without regret that he had quitted his native city; for he left behind him a fair and gentle girl whom he loved with tender affection, and in whom his heart had stored up its rich treasure of hope. She was his own niece; but mutual affection, no less than family reasons, had determined their union.

Alphonse Ratisbonne was a Jew; he was destined, to all appearance, to a brilliant position in the world, and had resolved to devote himself to the great work of the *regeneration* of his co-religionists. His thoughts and aspirations all revolved around this one high purpose, and his wrath kindled at every thing that reminded him of the curse that rests upon the descendants of Jacob. Fifteen years before the time of which I am speaking, and while he was yet a child, his heart had been wounded in one of its most sensitive affections. Theodore Ratisbonne, his brother, became a Catholic, and received holy orders. Time had been powerless to close this wound; his hatred deepened year by year, and he studiously fomented the deadly resentment of his family.

The blue sky of Naples could not make him forget the East, the object of his journey, nor the joys that awaited him on his return. But a few months remained, and Sicily, Malta, and Constantinople were to be visited. The summer of 1842 was to restore him to his home, and to witness a union which would fix his position in life, and assure his perfect happiness: it was time to be going. So he went out one morning to take his place in the steamer for Palermo. On his way it struck him that he had not seen Rome; that if he returned to Strasburg, and married, and became involved in the cares of business, there was but little likelihood of his ever revisiting Italy; and under the influence of this sudden thought he turned aside into the stage office took his place, and within three days found himself in Rome.

His stay was to be very short. His plans were all made; in a fortnight he would return to Naples. It was all in vain that the Eternal City displayed her wonders before him, he could not spare a day more; the East and his bride awaited him. So he set to work like a true tourist; visited ruins, churches, and galleries, and crowded his memory with a confused medley of impressions. He was eager to have done with this city, to which he had been drawn by an unaccountable fascination rather than by an intelligent curiosity.

And now he has finished his rounds. He starts for Naples to-morrow; but he must pay a farewell visit to an old friend. Gustave de Bussières had been his schoolfellow; and they had kept up their early friendship, in spite of the antagonism of their religious opinions. My brother Gustave is a very zealous Protestant, of the sect of the Pietists. He had made sundry attempts to gain over the young Israelite; but their discussions usually wound up with two expressions, which sufficiently indicate the position and temper of the disputants: *Fanatical Protestant*, shouted the one: *Callous Jew*, retorted the other.

Ratisbonne did not find my brother at home, and so he came on to me. But he had resolved not to come in; he would merely leave a farewell card. Chance, or rather Providence, ordered it so that his knock was answered by an Italian servant, who mistook his meaning, and introduced him, to his great annoyance, into the drawing-room.

We had met but once, at my brother's, and notwithstanding all my efforts, I had failed to obtain from Ratisbonne any thing beyond the cold civility of a well-bred man. However, he was Gustave's friend; he was the brother of my own dear friend, the Abbé Ratisbonne; and so I received him cordially, talked to him of the wonders around him, and gradually elicited his impressions of Rome.

"A rather odd thing happened to me the other day," said he, in passing; "while I was looking over the church of Aracœli on the Capitol, I felt myself suddenly seized with an emotion for which I could assign no cause. The *valet de place*, seeing my agitation, asked me what was the matter, and whether I would go out into the open air; adding, that he had often seen strangers similarly affected."

While Ratisbonne was telling me this, I suppose that my glistening eyes seemed to say to him, *You will be a Catholic;* for he went on to say, with a marked intention, that this emotion was not at all specifically Christian, but purely religious, in the most general sense of the word. "Besides," he continued, "as I came down from the Capitol a melancholy spectacle rekindled all my hatred of Catholicism: I passed through the Ghetto; and as I beheld the misery and the degradation of the Jews, I said to myself that, after all, it was a loftier thing to be on the side of the oppressed than on that of the oppressors." Our conversation now began to take a controversial turn; I tried, in my eager fervour, to impart to him my own Catholic convictions; but he only smiled at my efforts, said that he felt a sincere pity for my superstition, and that *he was born a Jew, and a Jew he would die.*

At this point of our discussion there came into my head a very extraordinary idea, suggested doubtless from above, for the wise of this world would have called it foolishness; I said:

"Since you are so confident in the strength and stability of your understanding, promise me to wear something that I will give you."

"Let me see it first; what sort of thing is it?"

"Only this medal," said I, and I held up to him a medal of the Blessed Virgin, at sight of which he threw himself back in his chair, with a gesture of mingled indignation and astonishment.

"But," said I, quietly, "from your point of view it must be perfectly indifferent to you, whereas it would give me the very greatest pleasure."

"Oh, I will not refuse you," he exclaimed, with a hearty laugh; "I shall at least show you that people have no right to accuse us Jews of obstinate and insurmountable infatuation. Besides, you are furnishing me with a charming chapter for my notes and impressions of my travels." And he went on with a succession of jests which wrung my heart, for to me they were so many blasphemies.

However, I threw round his neck a ribbon to which one of my daughters had attached the blessed medal while we were talking. And now there remained a point still more difficult to gain. I wished him to recite S. Bernard's pious invocation, *Memorare, o piissima Virgo*.... But this was too much for him; he refused very decidedly, and in a tone which seemed to say: Really, this man's impertinence is beyond all bounds. Still an interior force urged me on, and I combated his reiterated refusals with the energy of desperation. I held out the prayer to him, and begged him to take it away with him, requesting him to be kind enough to write it out for me, as I did not possess another copy of it.

At length he yielded, as if to rid himself of my importunity, and said, in a tone of vexation and contempt, "Well, I will write it out; you shall have my copy and I will keep yours;" and then he withdrew, muttering as he went, "What an unreasonable fellow that is! I wonder what he would say, if I were to plague him thus to make him recite some of my Jewish prayers!"

After he was gone, my wife and I looked at each other some time without speaking a word. Distressed by the blasphemy to which we had been compelled to listen, we united in imploring pardon from God for him, and we charged our two little daughters to say an *Ave Maria* at night for his conversion.

From this point every circumstance seems so important in order to the clear setting forth of this great work of God, that I feel it a duty to relate, as minutely and as accurately as I can, every thing that passed, from the day when Ratisbonne carried away the *Memorare* to the moment when the Mother of Mercy removed the veil which obstructed his soul's vision, and he received the grace to make a public profession of the Catholic faith.

At first Ratisbonne could not get over

his astonishment at my importunity: he, however, copied out the prayer; he read it and read it again, in order to discover what could give it such worth in my estimation, and why I ascribed to it so mighty an efficacy. By dint of writing and reading it he had got it by heart; it recurred to his memory continually; he went about repeating it mechanically, just as we unconsciously hum an air which has struck our fancy.

I, on my part, felt entirely absorbed in this result of my interview with a man of whom I knew next to nothing, and with whom I had conversed that day for the first time. I could not account for the internal force which impelled me towards him, and which inspired me with a deep inexplicable conviction that God would, sooner or later, open his eyes. I resolved to prevent, at all hazards, his departure from Rome. I went to pay him a visit at the Hôtel Serny; and as he was not within, I left a note for him, requesting him to call on me on the following day, which was Sunday, at about half-past ten in the morning.

In the evening it was my turn to watch before the Blessed Sacrament, according to he pious custom at Rome, in company with Prince M. A. B., and some other friends. begged them to join me in my prayers to obtain of God the conversion of a Jew.

Sunday, January 16th, 1842.

Ratisbonne came punctually at the hour appointed, and said to me, in an off-hand way, "Well, I hope you have forgotten yesterday's dreams. I am come to say good-bye to you; I am off to-night."

"My dreams! the thoughts which you are pleased to call dreams occupy me more than ever; and as to your going away, we will not speak of that, for you must absolutely put it off for a week."

"Oh, that is impossible; I have taken my place."

"What of that? We will go together to the office to say that you have changed your mind and are not going."

"Oh, now this is going too far; most decidedly I leave to-night."

"Most decidedly you will not leave to-night, even if I have to lock you up in my own room."

And then I went on to tell him that he could not leave Rome without having seen some grand ceremony at St. Peter's; that in a very few days he would have a very favourable opportunity; and, in short, he was so amazed at my pertinacity, that he suffered me to lead him off to the office to erase his name from the list of travellers; and then we visited the houses of the Augustinians and Jesuits.

I dined that same day at the Borghese palace, in company with the Count de Laferronnays; and in the course of the evening I told him the hopes that filled my own heart, and earnestly commended my young Jewish friend to his prayers. In the unreserved conversation that followed, M. de Laferronnays spoke to me of the confidence he had always felt in the protection of the Blessed Virgin, even at the time when the cares and distractions of political life had scarcely permitted that practical piety of which his later years offered so edifying an example. "Keep up a good hope," said he; "if he says the *Memorare*, you have him to a certainty, and many others with him."

Monday, January 17th, 1842.

I walked in different directions with Ratisbonne, who came to me about one o'clock. I was grieved to notice the little fruit of our conversations. He was still in the same disposition of mind—still hated Catholicism intensely, and made the most disparaging remarks about it—still parried by raillery, arguments which he thought not worth the trouble of serious refutation.

Mr. de Laferronnays died the same night at eleven o'clock. He left to his sorrowing friends and family the memory of an edifying example, and the consoling hope that God had called him thus because he was ripe for heaven.* Having long loved him as my own

---

* At the end will be found some details of the last moments of this truly noble and Christian man.

father, I had my part not only in the sorrow of his family, but in the mournful duties which devolved upon them; yet the thought of Ratisbonne followed me importunately even beside the bier of my friend.

Tuesday, January 18th, 1842.

I had passed part of the night with this sorrowing family, and felt unwilling to leave them; yet my thoughts turned restlessly to Ratisbonne, as though an unseen hand were drawing me towards him. I did not wish to leave the remains of my friend, but I could not banish from my mind this soul which I was so anxious to subdue to the faith. I communicated my mental conflict to the Abbé G., who had been for many years the chaplain and the friend of M. de Laferronnays. "Go," said he to me, "go and carry on the work you have begun; in doing so you will best fulfil the wishes of our deceased friend, who prayed fervently for the conversion of this young man."

I immediately ran after Ratisbonne, and took possession of him; I showed him various religious antiquities, that I might keep the great truths of Catholicism in contact with his mind. I got him to visit a second time the church of Aracœli. If he felt any return of his emotion it was very fugitive, for he listened coldly to me, and answered all my observations with witticisms. "I will turn over these things in my mind," said he, "when I am at Malta. I shall have plenty of time on my hands, for I am to spend two months there, and I shall be glad of any thing to keep me from *ennui*."

Wednesday, January 19th, 1842.

We walked in the direction of the Capitol and Forum. Close by, on the Cœlian hill, is the church of S. Stefano Rotondo, the walls of which are covered with frescoes, which represent with terrible fidelity the various torments of the early martyrs. Ratisbonne was horrified as we looked at them. "It is a hideous sight," said he, as though to anticipate my observations; "but those of your religion were quite as cruel to the poor Jews in the middle ages as the persecutors of antiquity were to the Christians."

I showed him at St. John Lateran the bas-reliefs above the statue of the twelve apostles. On one side are the figures of the Old Testament, on the other their fulfilment in the person of the Messias. The comparison seemed to him ingenious.

We continued our walk towards the villa Wolkonski. Ratisbonne was surprised at my calmness; he could not reconcile it with my eager desire for his conversion, and he remarked that he was more than ever a Jew. I answered that I was full of confidence in the promises of God, and that I was convinced that, since he was honest and sincere, would one day be a Catholic, even if an angel from heaven were necessary to enlighten him.

We were then passing by the Scala Santa; I took off my hat, and pointing to my companion, said, "Hail, Scala Santa, here is a man who will one day ascend you on his knees." Ratisbonne burst into a fit of laughter, and we separated without my being able to indulge the feeblest hope that I had, in any degree, shaken his convictions. But I believed Him who hath said: *Knock, and it shall be opened to you.* I returned to pray beside the remains of my beloved friend; and as I knelt I asked him to aid in the conversion of my young friend, if, as I hoped, he had already attained the rest of the blessed.

Thursday, January 20th, 1842.

Ratisbonne has not made the slightest advance towards the truth; his will is inflexible as ever, he turns every thing into ridicule, and seems to mind only earthly things About noon he went into a *café* on the Piazza di Spagna to read the newspapers. There he found my brother in-law, Edmund Humann; they chatted over the news of the day with a flippancy and an ease which excluded all idea of any serious preoccupation of mind.*

* It seems as if it had pleased Providence to order a..

It was about one o'clock. I had to make some arrangements at the church of S. Andrea delle Fratte for the ceremony of the morrow. But here is Ratisbonne coming down the Via Condotti; he will go with me, wait for me a few minutes, and then we will continue our walk. We entered the church. Ratisbonne noticed the preparations for a funeral, and asked for whom they were made. "For a friend I have just lost, and whom I loved exceedingly, Mr. de Laferonnays." He then began to walk about the nave, and his cold indifferent look seemed to say, "This is certainly a very ugly church." I left him on the epistle side of the church, to the right of a small enclosure destined to receive the coffin, and went into the convent.

I had only a few words to say to one of the monks—I wanted a tribune prepared for the family of the deceased; my absence could not have been more than ten or twelve minutes.

When I came back into the church I saw

things so as to exclude the possibility of doubt as to Ratisbonne's state of mind just before the unexpected grace of his conversion. About half-past twelve, as he came out of the café, he met his friend the Baron de Lotzbeck, and entered into conversation with him on matters the most frivolous. He spoke of dancing, of pleasure, of the fête given by Prince T. Had any one said to him at that moment, *Within two hours you will be a Catholic*, he would certainly have thought him out of his senses.

nothing of Ratisbonne for a moment; then I caught sight of him on his knees, in front of the chapel of S. Michael the Archangel. I went up to him, and touched him three or four times before he became aware of my presence. At length he turned towards me, his face bathed in tears; joined his hands, and said, with an expression which no words will render: "Oh, how this gentleman has prayed for me!"

I was quite petrified with astonishment; I felt what people feel in presence of a miracle. I raised Ratisbonne, I led him, or rather almost carried him, out of the church; I asked him what was the matter, and where he wished to go. "Lead me where you please," cried he; "after what I have seen I obey." I urged him to explain his meaning, but he could not; his emotion was too mighty and profound. He drew forth from his bosom the miraculous medal, and covered it with kisses and with tears. I brought him back to his apartment; and notwithstanding my repeated questions, I could get from him nothing but exclamations, broken by deep sobs: "Oh, what bliss is mine! how good is the Lord! what a fulness of grace and of happiness! how pitiable the lot of those who know not!" Then he burst into tears at thought of heretics and misbelievers. At length he asked me if I did not think him mad. "But no," he exclaimed,

"I am in my right senses; my God, my God, I am not beside myself; every one knows that I am not mad!"

This wild emotion became gradually more calm, and then Ratisbonne threw his arms around me and embraced me. His face was radiant, I might almost say transfigured; he begged me to take him to a confessor; wanted to know when he might receive holy baptism, for now he could not live without it; yearned for the blessedness of the martyrs whose sufferings he had seen depicted on the walls of S. Stefano Rotondo. He told me that he could give me no explanation of his state until he had received permission from a priest to do so; "for what I have to say," he added, "is something I can say only on my knees."

I took him immediately to the Gesù to see Father de Villefort, who begged him to explain himself. Then Ratisbonne drew forth his medal, kissed it, showed it to us, and exclaimed: "*I have seen her! I have seen her!*" and his emotion again choked his utterance. But soon he regained his calmness, and made his statement. I give it in his own words:

"I had been but a few moments in the church when I was suddenly seized with an unutterable agitation of mind. I raised my eyes, the building had disappeared from before me; one single chapel had, so to speak, gathered and concentrated all the light; and in the midst of this radiance I saw standing on the altar lofty, clothed with splendours, full of majesty and of sweetness, the Virgin Mary, just as she is represented on my medal. An irresistible force drew me towards her; the Virgin made me a sign with her hand that I should kneel down; and then she seemed to say, That will do! She spoke not a word, but I understood all."

Brief as this statement is, Ratisbonne could not utter it without pausing frequently to take breath, and to subdue the emotion with which he was thrilling. We listened to him with a sacred awe, mingled with joy and with gratitude, marvelling at the depth of the counsels of God, and at the ineffable treasures of His mercy. One word struck us especially by its depth of mystery: *She spoke not a word, but I understood all.* Indeed, it was quite enough to listen to Ratisbonne; the Catholic faith exhaled from his heart like a precious perfume from the casket, which contains it indeed, but cannot confine it. He spoke of the Real Presence like a man who believed it with all the energy of his whole being; but the expression is far too weak, he spoke like one to whom it was an object of *direct perception.*

On leaving Father de Villefort, we went to give thanks to God, first at S. Maria Maggiore, the favoured basilica of the Blessed Virgin, and then at S. Peter's.

It is impossible to convey an idea of the transport of Ratisbonne when he found himself in these churches. "Ah," said he to me, as he warmly pressed my hands, " now I understand the love with which Catholics regard their churches, and the piety which leads them to embellish and adorn them!... How good it is to be here! one would long to go no more out for ever!... it is earth no longer, it is the vestibule of heaven."

At the altar of the Blessed Sacrament, the Real Presence of Jesus so overwhelmed him that he was on the point of fainting; and I was obliged to lead him away, so awful did it seem to him to appear before the living God with the stain of original sin upon him. He hastened to take refuge in the chapel of the Blessed Virgin.* "Here," said he to me, " I can have no fear; I feel myself under the protection of an illimitable mercy."

He prayed with great fervour at the tomb of the holy apostles. The history of the conversion of S. Paul, which I related to him, made him shed tears abundantly.

He was astonished at the strength of the posthumous bond, to use his own expression, which united him to M. de Laferronnays; he wished to pass the night beside his remains— gratitude, he said, made it a duty. But Father de Villefort, seeing that he was exhausted

---

* Many may be glad to remark, that M. Ratisbonne was born in 1814, on the 1st of May, the month consecrated by Catholic piety to the Mother of Divine Grace.

with fatigue, prudently opposed this pious desire, and advised him not to remain later than ten o'clock.

Ratisbonne then told us that the night before he had not been able to sleep; that he had always before his eyes a large cross, of a peculiar form, and without the image of our Saviour. "I made," said he, "incredible efforts to drive away this figure; but they were all fruitless." Some hours later his eye casually fell on the reverse of the miraculous medal, and he recognised his cross.

Meanwhile I was impatient to return to the family of M. de Laferronnays: I had such consolation to give them, at the moment when the venerated remains of him whom they bewailed were about to be taken from before their eyes. I entered the chamber of death in a state of agitation, I might almost say of joy, which at once attracted the attention of all present, and showed them that I had something of importance to communicate. They all followed me into an adjoining room, and I hastily related all that had passed.

I had brought them tidings from heaven. Their tears of grief were in a moment changed into tears of gratitude. These poor, smitten hearts could now bear with perfect Christian resignation that keenest of sacrifices, which death exacts, the last farewell to the remains of him they had loved.

But I was eager to see again the son

whom God had just given me; he had begged me not to leave him alone; he felt that he needed a friend into whose heart he could pour out the unfathomable emotions of such a day.

I asked him again and again the circumstances of the miraculous vision. He was quite unable to explain how he had passed from the right side of the church to the chapel, which is on the left, and from which he was separated by the preparations that had been made for the funeral service. All he knew was, that he had found himself suddenly on his knees, and prostrate close to this chapel. At first he had been enabled to see clearly the Queen of Heaven, in all the splendour of her immaculate beauty; but he could not sustain the radiance of that divine light. Thrice he had tried to gaze once more on the Mother of Mercy; thrice he proved his inability to raise his eyes beyond her blessed hands, from which there flowed, in luminous rays, a torrent of graces.

"O my God!" cried he, "I who but half an hour before was blaspheming still! I who felt a hatred so deadly of the Catholic religion! . . . But all who know me know well enough that, humanly speaking, I have the strongest reasons for remaining a Jew. My family is Jewish, my bride is a Jewess, my uncle is a Jew. . . . In becoming a Catholic, I sacrifice all the interests and all the hopes I have on earth; and yet I am not mad— every one knows that I am not mad, that I have never been mad! Surely they must receive my testimony."

Friday, January 21st, 1842.

The news of this signal miracle began to spread through Rome.* People were running from house to house, questioning one another, relating to one another the imperfect details they had been able to gather. It was all in vain that, with customary caution, they were on their guard lest they should receive a statement so startling on insufficient testimony. Doubt soon became impossible in presence of facts so evident and so notorious. Every one seemed to bless God for the privilege of being in Rome at a time when it had pleased Him to quicken our confidence in the immaculate Virgin, by attesting in so wonderful a way the power of her intercession. Every one longed to see and to question the thrice-happy youth, for whom the Mother of Divine Grace had descended from heaven to earth.

* Yesterday morning, as we were taking our colazione in haste, before visiting *S. Agnese fuòri le Mure*, our good Monica came running in to tell us, in the joy of her heart, the news, *Un Ebreo è convertito!*—a Jew was converted yesterday; yes, here, in our church of S. Andrea delle Fratre! *Gesù mio! che bel miraculo!* We could not stay to hear more. In the evening this conversion was the topic of conversation at Cardinal Pacca's; and this morning I heard all the details of this striking event. I met M. de Bussières in the *salon* of the Countess K., and he was good enough to relate to us what he has since published."—*Gaume; les trois Rome,* ii. 173.

I was with Ratisbonne at Father Villefort's, when General Chlapouski was introduced. "Sir," said he, "so you have seen the likeness of the Blessed Virgin; tell me all about it."

"The likeness, sir!" cried Ratisbonne, interrupting him; "the likeness! I have seen her herself, in reality, in her own person, just as I see you there before me."

I cannot refrain from observing here, that even if we can imagine an illusion in the case of a person of Ratisbonne's character and education, with prejudices so violent, and with such interests both of affection and of position, it could not have been produced or aided by any outward representation; for in the chapel which was the scene of the miracle, there is no statue, or picture, or image of the Blessed Virgin, of any kind.

I was anxious now that Ratisbonne should be introduced to the family of M. de Laferronnays. The most critical event of his life was so bound up with the bereavement which weighed so sorely upon them, that it seemed but right that he should alleviate their sorrow, by telling them with his own lips of the tie of everlasting gratitude wherewith it had pleased God to link his soul with that of their departed one. But he was too much affected to talk consecutively; he could do little more than press with an indescribable agitation the hands which were stretched out to him, as to a brother or to a beloved child. "Oh, believe me, believe my words," said he repeatedly, when they questioned him; "it is to the prayers of M. de Laferronnays that I owe my conversion."

The new convert spent at my house the few days that passed before the retreat, in which he was to be prepared for his baptism. He read me some parts of his letters to his bride, to his uncle, to all the members of his family; so that I was enabled to read his soul to its lowest depth. In our private conversations he recurred continually to the manifest proofs, which ought to convince the most sceptical, of the miraculous intervention by which his conversion was effected, and of his own perfect sincerity.

"The weightiest inducements," said he, "the strongest interests, bound me to my religion. A man has a claim to be believed when he sacrifices every thing to a conviction which must have come from heaven. . . If all that I have stated is not rigorously true, I commit a crime, not only the most daring, but the most senseless and motiveless. In making my entrance into Catholicism by a sacrilegious lie, I not only risk my position in this world, but I lose my soul, and assume the frightful responsibility of all those whom my example may induce to do as I am doing. And what interest can I have in this? Alas, when my brother became a Catholic, and a priest, I persecuted him with a more unrelenting fury than any other member of my family. We were completely sundered; I hated him with a virulent hatred, though he had fully pardoned me. At the time of my betrothal, I said to myself that it was fitting that I should be reconciled with my brother; I wrote him a few cold lines, to which he returned an answer full of tenderness and of charity. . . .

"One of my nephews died eighteen months ago. My brother, the abbé, wished to baptise him; when I knew it, I was in a frenzy of rage. . . . I trust that God may send me the severest of tests, that His own glory may be advanced, and that the world may know that I am sincere."

And surely we cannot question the sincerity and good faith of the man who, in his twenty-eighth year, sacrifices all the joys of his heart, all the hopes of his life, at the call of conscience. For he knew well all the consequences of his resolution; he knew that Christianity is the worship of the Cross; again and again he had been told of the trials which awaited him, and of the duties laid upon him by the religion which he was so eager to embrace.

From the moment in which he requested the sacrament of baptism, he was placed under the care of the venerable father who rules a society justly dear to every Christian. This good father, after hearing his story with his wonted benignity, and at the same time with calm gravity, had urged him to weigh well the sacrifices he would be compelled to make, the serious obligations he would have to fulfil, the peculiar conflicts which awaited him, the temptations and testing trials to which a step like his would expose him; and then, pointing to a crucifix which stood on the table, he said:

"That cross which you saw in your sleep, when once you have been baptised, you must not only worship it, but you must bear it;" and then, opening the Holy Scriptures, he turned to the second chapter of Ecclesiasticus, and read to Ratisbonne these words:

"Son, when thou comest to the service of God, stand in justice and in fear, and prepare thy soul for temptation. Humble thy heart and endure: incline thine ear, and receive the words of understanding: and make not haste in the time of clouds. Wait on God with patience; join thyself to God, and endure, that thy life may be increased in the latter end. Take all that shall be brought upon thee: and in thy sorrow endure, and in thy humiliation keep patience. For gold and silver are tried in the fire, but acceptable men in the furnace of humiliation. Believe God, and He will recover thee: and direct thy way, and trust in Him. Keep His fear, and grow old therein."

These divine words produced a deep impression on Ratisbonne. Far from discouraging him, they strengthened his resolution, and gave him very serious and sober ideas of Christianity. He listened, however, in silence; but at the close of the retreat which preceded his baptism, he went in the evening to see the holy priest who had read him these words a week before, and begged for a copy of them, that he might preserve them, and meditate on them every day of his life.

Such are the facts which I submit to the consideration of all thoughtful men. I have related them artlessly, in their own simplicity, in all their truthfulness; for the edification of those who believe, for the instruction of those who are yet seeking the place of their rest. And happy shall I deem myself, if, after having wandered long, too long, in the gloom and amidst the contradictions of Protestant sects, I may, by this simple narrative, excite in some erring brother the will to cry, with the blind man in the Gospel, *Lord, that my eyes may be opened!* for every one who truly prays will soon have his eyes opened to the sunlight of Catholic truth.*

---

* "My brother, two hours after his conversion, was seen by Cardinal Mezzofanti, who was ready to throw himself on his knees in adoration to God. Nothing was known of my brother at Rome, and at first great apprehensions were entertained as to what his character might turn out to be. *He had never read two pages of the Bible, never received any religious instruction whatever,* was altogether of a light and superficial character The Blessed Virgin appeared to him as close as I

THE BAPTISM.

Monday, January 31st, 1842.

Those whose privilege it was to obtain admission to the church of the Jesuits to-day, will not readily forget the ceremony which has completed that extraordinary event which still so profoundly affects the whole city, and which publicly authenticated one of those marvels of grace by which God would revive the faith of the lukewarm, and allure into the right way those who are yet walking in darkness.

M. Ratisbonne has made to-day, in presence of the Cardinal Vicar, his profession of the Catholic faith; he has received holy baptism, has been confirmed, and has made his first communion.

Long before the appointed hour the church of the Gesù, which had been chosen by the Cardinal Vicar for the ceremony, was filled with a pious crowd, eager to see this young Jew, whom the immaculate Virgin herself has

---

am to you; she made a motion to him that he should remain quiet under the divine influence. On rising out of his ecstasy, *he had received intuitively the knowledge of the Christian faith.* ... I believe that he has more than once received a repetition of the grace he had at Rome, but I have never asked him on the subject.... My uncle is worth from six to seven millions of francs; he has disinherited my brother, who has renounced every thing.

"M. L'ABBÉ THÉODORE RATISBONNE."
Allies' Journal in France, p. 44.

deigned to bring to the foot of the cross. There were present also many of those wandering sheep, those curious persons who long to see every thing that is novel and striking; but a contagious reverence pervaded the congregation, and all hearts were for a time fused into a oneness of emotion by the interest and awe inspired by the distinguished proselyte.

Prudent precautions had been taken to preserve that degree of order which was necessary for the common edification of all. The space between the altar of St. Ignatius and that of St Francis Xavier was prepared for the accommodation of the large assemblage; and although there were no places reserved, the zeal of true Catholics had forestalled the eagerness of the merely curious, and thrown around the altar the protection of their reverent silence and devout prayers.

About half-past eight M. Ratisbonne, clothed in the white robe of a catechumen, was led in by the reverend Father Villefort, who had prepared him for baptism, and by Baron Théodore de Bussières, his sponsor, and took his place in the chapel of St. Andrew, near the principal entrance of the church.* During the half-hour which fol-

* "To-day we took part in a ceremony, or rather an event, the memory of which will never fade away from my heart—the baptism of M. Ratisbonne. Ten days only had passed since his conversion; but the marvellous neophyte

lowed, he was naturally the object of general curiosity; but he endured with perfect resignation this severe test, so trying at a moment when his heart was heaving with the yearning presentiments of a new life. From time to time he fervently pressed the rosary which he held in his hand, or gazed on the medal attached to it, as if to seek in the thought of her whose intercession had saved him, the strength and courage he so much needed.

At nine o'clock, his Eminence Cardinal Patrizi, Vicar of his Holiness, began to recite the prayers prescribed in the ritual for the baptism of adults. There are found psalms which seem as though they had been written expressly to clothe with words the feelings of the catechumen, and to tell out the way in which the Lord had been pleased to call him to the truth. For so wondrous is the depth of the Holy Scriptures, that every one finds in them the expressions which render most aptly the ever-varying experience of his soul, and the manifold circumstances of his inner life.

had understood all, and the illustrious Cardinal Mezzofanti, who is charged with the examination of catechumens, was amazed at the plenitude of light which the Father of lights had so instantaneously poured into this privileged soul.... What a spectacle! M. de Bussières, a converted Protestant, leading a Jew into the bosom of a Catholic Church! and what a Jew! a *jeune France* of eight-and-twenty, in all the fulness of his powers, his reason, and his self-will; but yesterday godless, mocking, blaspheming, and to-day gentle as a lamb...."— Gaume; *les trois Rome*, ii. 220.

And what could paint more vividly the troubled and weary heart of the young Jew, as he beheld the enchantment pass away from the face of earth, and was sad amidst the pleasures of his favoured position? *Why art thou cast down, O my soul?* Poor stricken soul, in vain dost thou shift thine horizon, and seek the distraction of thy sadness in other and strange lands; still will *thy tears be thy bread day and night*, for there is no resting-place for the exile,—for day by day it is said to thee, in thy secret heart, *where is now thy God?* But *hope thou in God;* for soon shalt thou confess His Holy Name, and find the heart's true rest, the balm for every wound: *hope thou in God; for I will still give praise to Him, the salvation of my countenance, and my God.* Think, that in His own appointed time He hath sent unto thee the Mother of mercies: *in the day-time the Lord hath commanded His mercy.* Hope thou, then, in God; fear no longer to draw near unto the tabernacle of awe wherein lies hidden the Holy of Holies; say thou rather in thine heart, *and I will go in to the altar of God;* He alone can slake my soul's deep thirst. Thou feelest now the hideousness of sin, of thine own inherited taint; *when shall I come, when shall I enter the sacred ark, out of which is no salvation? when may I cast myself down before the face of my God? when shall I come and appear before the presence of God?*

Like as the hart panteth after the fountains of water, so longeth my soul for the hallowed streams of baptism, so thirsteth my soul for God, the spring and fount of all strength and of all life.

When these preliminary prayers were said, his Eminence proceeded in procession to the lower end of the church. There Father Villefort and M. de Bussières presented to him the young Jew. "What cravest thou of the Church of God?" "Faith." And this faith, this holy Catholic faith, it was his already; the bright and morning star had already risen upon him, and enlightened him with its clear shining. And thus, when commanded to "detest the perfidy of the Jews, to put away with contempt the superstition of the Hebrews," he knew not a moment's hesitation, and the meek firmness of his replies showed that he was not unworthy of the boon the Church accorded him, in abridging for him the tests appointed for catechumens.

Already has the bishop breathed thrice upon him to put to flight the spirit of evil; he has marked him with the Christian's characteristic mark, the venerable sign of the cross, on his forehead, on his eyes, on his ears, on his breast, on his shoulders; in order to impress upon the new-born Christian that it was henceforth his duty to hallow to Christ his intelligence and his heart, and to bear with loving readiness the yoke of the cross. He has given him to taste the salt of wisdom, and has said over him the prayers of exorcism. The neophyte is prostrate on the threshold of the temple—a last, surest evidence of submission, a last, unlooked-for test is applied, "Kiss the dust;" and calmly and unhesitatingly he obeys. There is no doubt that he is a Christian indeed, for his heart has intuitively discerned that humility is the strait gate which leadeth to truth and to salvation. Lesson of wondrous eloquence for us all, who are but too prone to forget that Jesus our Master was *meek and lowly in heart.*

There is no doubt; the *mind that was in Christ* is in this candidate for Christ's service too, for he is lowly and submissive. The Church hesitates no longer; she looks upon him, she treats him as her own beloved child. She remembers no more his life in times past, nor his blasphemies of yesterday; she beholds in him only the privileged child of Mary's adoption. The bishop places the end of his stole in his hand, in token of adoption, to teach him that in the Catholic family the children must lean trustfully on their fathers; and thus he leads, as in triumph, this beloved sheep of the fold, snatched from the jaws of the destroyer, to the altar of St. Ignatius.

But how shall we render justice to the emotion of the congregation as Ratisbonne passed before them? His face characterised by a happy blending of decision and of gentleness, his long beard, his measured step, his white garment, every thing carried them back in thought to the days of the primitive Church—the Church of the catacombs.

Some worthy Roman women, who were crushing me in order to see more clearly, well expressed in their own simple way the brotherly charity which animated all who were present: *Ah, quanto sei caro! ah, beato lui!* and then they kissed their rosaries as if to thank the cause of our joy for this triumph of grace.

Then they pointed with affectionate curiosity to him whom God deigned to use to prepare His way before His face: "See he is a Frenchman—it was he who gave the medal to the Jew, who made him pray to the Blessed Virgin. *Ma che buon signore! che Dio le benedica!*" And we too repeated their words, and said in our deepest hearts: May God bless him, and all that are his!

And now the bishop is standing near the altar, and the catechumen kneels before him to receive the sacred waters of baptism. He is asked his name. "Marie," is his reply, with an outburst of gratitude and of love Marie! the thrice-blessed name of the Queen of Patriarchs, who has opened to him the gates of the Church, and will open for him those of heaven—the everlasting gates.

"What crave you?"
"Baptism."

"Do you renounce the devil?"
"I renounce him.
"And all his pomps?"
"I renounce them."
"And all his works?"
"I renounce them."
"Do you believe in God the Father Almighty, Creator of heaven and earth?"
"I believe in Him."
"Do you believe in Jesus Christ His only Son our Lord, who was born and who suffered for us?"
I believe in Him."
"Do you believe in the Holy Ghost, the Holy Catholic Church, the Communion of Saints, the remission of sins, the resurrection of the flesh, and the life everlasting?"
"I do believe."

The tone and accent of deepest conviction with which this child of Mary pronounced this profession of the Catholic faith, produced on all present an impression which still thrills throughout their whole being.

"And now, what desirest thou?"
"Baptism."

At length that sacred flood whose waters spring up unto everlasting life, has come down upon that brow so lowly bent; Marie Ratisbonne rises up a Christian,—a Christian pure and fervent as are the angels who stand about the throne of God.

He holds in his hand the blessed taper, whose flame betokens that light of submissive faith which wavers not nor misleads. The laying on of hands and the unction with holy chrism impart to him a second grace, in confirming the fulness of that which he has already received. Henceforward Ratisbonne is a disciple of the cross; he is prepared to confess aloud to all the faith of that Jesus who gave Himself for us.

And then M. l'Abbé Dupanloup[*] addressed to the congregation some of those glowing words which rise so readily from his heart when he has to tell of the goodness of our God, or of the loving power of Mary. We give a few fragments—fragments, alas! very incomplete and very weak —of this fervid *improvisation*. The sacred orator avowed before all his full and entire faith in the miraculous intervention of Mary, in the sudden conversion for which they were now blessing God; avoiding, as beseemed a submissive son of the Church, every expression which might even seem to anticipate the regular decision of the one only competent authority on a question of miraculous agency.

[*] Now Bishop of Orleans.

EXTRACTS FROM THE DISCOURSE OF M. DUPANL UP.

The providence of God is wondrous in all its designs and in all its methods, and deeply are they to be pitied who can neither comprehend nor extol it. For them the life of man is but a mournful mystery; his days but a chain whose links are twined by fate; and man himself but a creature, noble indeed, but accursed in every faculty, thrust forth far from heaven upon this earth of tears and lamentation, to live in gloom, to die in despair, utterly forgotten by a God who heeds neither his virtues nor his sorrows.... But, O my God, Thou art not thus unheeding, neither hast thou thus fashioned us; notwithstanding our profound and infinite misery, we are not to this extent miserable: Thy providence still keepeth watch over us; higher than highest heavens, deeper far and wider than the great and wide sea; it is an abyss unfathomable, of power, and wisdom, and of love..... Thou hast made us for Thyself, O Lord, and our hearts are restless until they find rest in Thee. There is within us a sense of need, deep, infinite, which sways our whole souls, which devours us,..... and whenever we follow the instinctive tendency of this mighty want we surely find Thee..... I bless Thee, above all, I adore Thee for that from Thy lofty and eternal dwelling-place

Thou dost remember, and remember with compassion, the creatures Thy hand hath formed; for that from Thy heavens Thou dost design a look of pity and of love on us, the lowliest product of Thine almighty hand; for that, as saith the Prophet, Thou dost shake the heavens and the earth, and multiply Thy prodigies, in order to save those whom Thou lovest so well.... to subdue to Thyself one solitary soul.....

And you, on whom every eye is now turned with unutterable tenderness—for it is God, it is the mercy of God, that we see and love in you—you, whose presence here inspires my thoughts—tell us what were your thoughts and the ways of your heart,..... by what hidden ways of mercy the Lord has followed you, brought you back.....

For who are you? what is your petition in this holy place? what homage do you come to pay? what means that robe of stainless white you bear? Tell us whence you came, and whither your steps were bent? and what power has so suddenly changed your purposes?.... Tell us how, like Abraham, your great ancestor,—Abraham, whose true son you have this day become,—you were going on, following the voice of the Lord, but not knowing whither you went; your eyes yet sealed in darkness until you reached the Holy City. ..... The work of the Lord has not yet reached its accomplishment; but it is yours to tell us by what degrees the Sun of truth and of justice arose upon your soul,—what was its glowing dawn..... Why is it that you feel with us, more keenly perhaps than we feel, the good word of grace, the powers of the world to come, and all our hopes so full of blessedness?.... Tell us, for we have the right to ask, why do you thus enter into our possession, as into your own heritage? Who has placed you thus at home in our midst? for yesterday you were but a stranger and a sojourner with us; we knew you not—or rather we knew you......

Here let me utter all; for I know what joy I shall infuse into your heart in setting up this memorial of your misery, and of the mercies of our God.

You loved not the truth, though He who is the truth loved you; you resisted the efforts of the most fervid and the purest zeal with a smile of disdain, or a contemptuous silence, or a subtle quibble, or a haughty demand of overwhelming evidence, and, alas! with blasphemous jests. O God most patient! O Thou who lovest us in spite of our sins and our miseries! Thy mercy has oftentimes a depth, a sublimity, a tenderness, a might and a delicacy, which are to us infinite and incomprehensible.

Suddenly a rumour spreads throughout the Holy City, and diffuses consolation throughout all Christian hearts. He who yesterday was a blasphemer, who, even this very morning, ridiculed the friends of God—he preacheth the Gospel—grace from above has been poured upon his lips; from his mouth proceed only blessing and words of gentleness; the keenest light of faith has shone on his eyes; the unction of the Holy One has taught him all things. Whence has he acquired those enlightened eyes of the soul, which see all, which have *understood all?* O God, Thou art good; Thy goodness is infinite; and I love to repeat those gracious words which we heard so recently from the blessed lips of him whose memory can never fade away from our hearts; —we made lamentation for him but a few days since, but now we regret him indeed, yet we cannot grieve for him: " Yes, Thou art good, and the children of men have done well to call Thee the *good* God." * Thou shakest the laws of nature; Thou deemest nothing too great for the salvation of Thy children. When Thou comest not Thyself, Thou sendest Thine angels..... Thine angels, did I say?... O my God, shall I speak? a reverent reserve should close my lips—but *quæ est ista*—who is this? Silence and speech are alike impossible.

Hail Mary, full of grace! and thou lovest to shower down on us the plenitude of thy mother's heart. *The Lord is with thee!* It

---

* The last words of M. de Laferronnays.

is through thee that He has been pleased to come down even unto us. And now it behooves me to borrow the kindling utterances of prophets, or to range the courts of heaven in quest of images to set forth thy dignity and thy praise. For, O Mary, thy name is sweeter to us than earth's purest joy, sweeter than its choicest odours, ravishing beyond the harmony of angels, *in corde jubilus;* sweeter to the believing heart than the honeycomb to the lips of the weary traveller, *mel in linguâ;* more helpful and gentler to the guilty heart, when it repents, than is the dew of evening to the leaves which the scorching heats of noon have withered, *ros in herbâ.* Thou art fair as the orb of night, *pulchra ut luna;* and it is thou who settest again in the right way the feet of the wandering traveller; thou art brilliant as the dawn, *aurora consurgens;* mild and pure as the star of morn, *stella matutina;* and it is thou who dost herald the rising of the Sun of justice in our hearts.

O Mary, I fail in power to show forth thy greatness and thy manifold claims to our love, and it is a joy to me to sink back overpowered by a glory so vast. But since I am speaking in the congregation of thy children, who are also my brethren, I will utter without fear the thoughts of my heart in regard of thy praise.

At thy name, O Mary, the heavens rejoice, and earth sings for gladness of heart, while hell shudders in impotent wrath. None can truly invoke thine aid and perish. The stately temples reared by mighty nations, the gold, the banners wrought by royal hands, and the humble thank-offerings laid by the mariner on the threshold of some lowly chapel, the homage of highest art and the rude image traced by martyr hands on some wall of the catacombs,—all alike attest thy power to still every storm that perils the heart of man, and to draw down on us the mercy of our God. Mary, I have seen the wildest spots of earth smile at thy name and put on gracefulness; the pious dwellers in the far-off wilderness sing thy glories; the echoing mountains and the ever-sounding torrents are vocal with thy praises. I have seen, in earth's most stately cities, the purest and noblest virtues flourish under the shadow of thy name; I have seen the thought of thee and the pure joy of thy feasts preferred to earth's most winning fascinations..... I have seen old men, after sixty, eighty years of a life void of faith and of virtue, rise on the bed of sickness; remember, at sound of thy name, the God who had crowned their infancy with blessings; and thou didst beam upon their dying eyes as a pledge of safety and of everlasting peace...... O Mary, who art thou, then? *Quæ est ista?* Thou art the Mother of our Saviour; and Jesus God over all, blessed for evermore, is the fruit of thy womb; thou art our sister, soror *nostra es;* daughter of Adam, thou hast no part in our fatal heritage, and our woes elicit thy deepest, tenderest commiseration.

O Mary, thou art the noblest creation of he power of God. Thou art the most winning levice of His goodness. Thou art the sweetest smile of His mercy. O God, open the eyes of those who see not, that they may see Mary, and know the sweet radiance of her mother's eyes. Touch the hearts which love her not; for to faith there is but one step from Mary to the Eternal Word, to that beauty ever old, yet ever new; to that uncreated light which healeth our blinded eyes and satisfieth our largest desires, from Mary to Jesus, from the Mother to the Son.

Brother well-beloved,—and I am happy in being the first to greet you by this name,—you see under what favourable auspices you make your entry into this new Jerusalem, which is the dwelling-place of God,—into *the Church of the living God, which is the pillar and ground of the truth* ..... But before I allow your heart to expand to the fulness of joys which await it, there is a solemn lesson for you to-day; and, as I am the first to cause you to hear the joyful sound of the Gospel, I dare not hide from you its most austere teaching. You have understood all, you tell us; but permit me to ask you, have you understood the mystery of the cross? ..... Take good heed —it is the basis and ground-work of Christianity.

I do not mean now that hallowed cross which you lovingly revere, because it brings before you Jesus crucified in expiation of your sins. Let me borrow the energetic language of an ancient apologist of our faith, and say to you: We are not now concerned with the cross which it is so blessed to revere, but of that cross which you must learn to bear. *Ecce cruces jam non adorandæ, sed subeundæ.* This is what you must thoroughly understand, if you are a Christian; and this is what your baptism has already taught you......

Moreover, it were vain to attempt to conceal it, it can scarcely be that your future life should offer you no cross to be borne. I see them preparing; undoubtedly you must revere them from afar, but there is something better than that—you must accept them when they come near and endure them with good courage. I am greatly deceived if patience be not the appointed means of increasing and strengthening your faith, and enabling you to bring forth its fruits. And bless God for it. You have been brought within the Christian Church by Mary and by the Cross. It is an introduction of good augury. Blessed be God for it! for I know He has given you ears to hear and a heart to understand this language. Son of the Catholic Church, you will share the destiny of your Mother! Look out on Rome, the spot on which you have just been new-born unto God! Continuous conflict and continuous triumph—this is her earthly heritage; and thus nothing appals by its novelty, after eighteen centuries of warfare and of victory......

It is at the very centre of Catholic unity, at the footstool of the highest apostolical chair, whence flash forth the keenest purest rays of the faith to pierce the darkness of paganism, heresy, and judaism, that the Church has poured on your brow the saving stream of regeneration. It is Peter himself, that Moses of the new law, worthily represented by the first vicar of his illustrious successor, who has smitten for you the rock of wonder, the immovable stone: *Petra erat Christus*, whence flows that water which springeth up unto eternal life. It is in the living flame of the Holy Ghost that you have been baptised: *Spiritu Sancto et igne*. The splendours of the noblest ceremonies of our religion fall full upon you, and we who are round about you catch some gleams of their glory. It is to-day your Pentecost, and the Spirit of might and of love hath filled your heart! It is to-day your Paschal time, and Jesus Christ is about to feed you with His sacred Flesh and with His precious Blood. It is He Himself whom you will receive, really, substantially, and truly; your faith, your emotion, the tears which stream from your eyes, anticipate all

I would say. Fear not that I shall weary you now with long and insipid exposition and proof of a truth which it is your high blessedness to believe. I will say but one word, which you will feel to be true,—Jesus Christ is far too truly our God and our friend that He should feed our souls with an empty figure, and cheat our love with a baseless illusion; besides, we need Him thus; for He commands us to love Him so as to be ready to lay down our lives for Him, and the Divine Eucharist has ever been the food and the strength of martyrs. Hear what Christian antiquity hath believed and hath handed down......

But I pause, for I am retarding your blessedness. Now, at this moment, the eyes of heaven look lovingly down upon you, and earth gives you its added blessing, and Jesus Christ awaits you. Go forward, then—the angels of God have begun this glad rejoicing, and the children of God echo it along here in earth; and he who seemed to our eyes to die, and whose spirit liveth in the hands of the Lord, you know that his desires and his prayers have not been wanting—the solemn moment is come.

Abraham, Isaac, and Jacob, patriarchs and prophets cheer you on from out of heaven; and Moses gives you his blessing, because the law written in your heart hath met and recognised the Gospel; mercy and truth uphold you, justice and peace compass you round about, repentance and innocence crown you with gladness; and it is Mary who receives you and who protects you.

O Mary, it is an imperious want of our hearts, no less than a duty, to utter yet once again the prayer to which we owe, it may be, the consolations of this happy day. And throughout this vast assembly, behold, with one heart and one voice we say:

"Remember, O Mary, Virgin most pitiful, that it has never been heard from old time that any one who has fled to thy protection, implored thine aid, and sought thine intercesson, has been left desolate. Groaning beneath the burden of our sins, we come, O Virgin of virgins, to cast ourselves into thine arms. O Mother of the Word, remember now those who stand in grace, those who are in sin; remember now those who know thee, and those who know thee not; remember now all our miseries, and all thy tender pity. I will not say: Remember this youth; for he is thy child, and the blessed and glorious conquest of thy love; but I will say to thee: Remember those friends so dear, for whom he offers thee this day the first prayers of his Catholic heart; restore them to him in time, restore them to him in eternity......

And since I am a stranger here,—but no, there are no strangers at Rome—every

Catholic is a Roman,—but since we were both born on the soil of France, I know that I do but give utterance to the desires of all hearts here present when I say to thee: Remember France: it has still noble virtues, generous souls, heroic self-devotedness. Bring back again upon the Church of France the fair beauty of the days of old.

The holy sacrifice of the Mass closed the ceremony. It was scarcely possible to witness without a quickening of faith, the fervour with which the new convert prayed, and the silent recollectedness with which all the congregation united their prayers to his. It was especially at the solemn moment of communion that our Lord seemed to pour down His sweetness and His graces upon the pious multitude. Our dear brother Ratisbonne was so annihilated by his consciousness of the Divine Presence, that it was necessary to support him as he drew near to the holy table; and after having received the Bread of angels, he was unable to rise without the aid of Father Villefort and of his sponsor. His tears flowed abundantly; he was quite overcome by the depth and complexity of his emotions, and by the ineffable graces with which our Lord filled his soul.

To see this young man, but a few days before an obstinate Jew, and now a Catholic glowing with faith and charity, one could not help saying to one's self; O Lord, Thou art wonderful in all Thy works. And the profound exclamation of the convert was ever present to our thoughts: *I understood all.*

A large number of persons gave the young convert the truest proof of their brotherly love, by following him to the holy table. This pious communion in our Lord was most edifying, and gave to the whole ceremony a character of fervour and of love.

In this sacred banquet, in which the chosen friends of God celebrated the ever-new miracle of his mercy, every heart was joined in love to the family that was sorrowing beneath the visitation of God's hand. The thought of the beloved and venerable man whose departure from earth they mourned, threw a reflection of the heavenly glory over this pious solemnity. *O, how this gentleman has prayed for me!* were Ratisbonne's words, at the moment when the veil fell from his eyes, and when he knew nothing of this fervent Christian but that he had passed from earth. O Lord, I adore the depth of Thy councils. The prophet-king asked of old; Shall the dust of the tomb give thanks unto Thy name, and declare Thy truth? Yes, Lord, for Thou hast heard the prayer of the righteous man, and Thou hast poured down with full hands Thy consolations, into the wounds and sorrows of earth, that we may learn to give glory to Thy name; and not allow ourselves to sink into despondency; *Ut cantet tibi gloria mea, et non compunger.*

And now it was finished and done. Ratisbonne has been admitted to all the joys, to all the graces of Catholic life. Blessed be God who hath given us yet another brother; the voice of joy and of thanksgiving is in the dwellings of the just; the song of triumph peals to the vault of the temple; the restrained emotion of every heart finds utterance. *Te Deum laudamus!* we praise Thee, O God! shouted the congregation in one ecstatic burst: we praise *Thee.* And then we began to feel, with a thrill of joyful mirth, what is the communion of saints. Those manifold voices, mingled in one triumphal shout of gratitude, gave us a foretaste of the blessedness of heaven. The heart that could remain cold and unmoved amidst the enthusiasm of this sublime shout was surely not the heart of a Catholic.

After the *Te Deum*, the cardinal led the new-born child of the Church into the house of the Jesuits: and it is said, that when they had left the sacred building, he could not constrain his emotion, but pressed to his heart with paternal tenderness him whose feet he had set in the way of life.

Ratisbonne's joy was indescribable. Surrounded by a crowd of persons eager to see him, to hear him, to embrace him, he received the congratulations of all with a bounding gladness of heart at being now a son of the holy Catholic family.

An eye-witness relates, that when at length he retired to the cell he had occupied during his retreat, his first act was to prostrate himself before his crucifix, to thank the Saviour of the world for the graces which had been vouchsafed to him.

And as for those whose privilege it was to be present at this glorious ceremony, they went away with this consoling truth graven on their inmost hearts: that when a man seeks God sincerely, He soon cometh, even though a miracle be needed to make plain His way before Him.

When God, in His fatherly tenderness, bestows on His children some of those extraordinary favours which rekindle faith and flood the heart with a love passing all understanding, they feel as if they would make here their tents amidst the delights of this interior joy, and prolong and retain all that has contributed to it—all that may perpetuate it.

In order to satisfy the pious desire of devout souls, we will linger yet awhile beside the happy child of Mary; we will follow his steps and listen to his words from the thrice-blessed day when he was united to us by partaking of the holiest of mysteries, to the time when this account is given to the world.

And he, too—he longed to abide on that Thabor. Object of such rare and abundant grace; having thrown far from him, like a garment worn out, the miseries of his past life; adorned in that baptismal innocence, which, alas, so soon contracts stain in the world, he pined for solitude, dreaded the throng of men, evaded the eager curiosity of all, and, as it were, set a seal upon his heart, lest any of the treasures confided to him by God should be lost.

He manifested, then, a great desire to pass in retreat the days of dissipation which were drawing near. With what eye would he gaze upon the fond pleasures and vain joys of earth; he, to whom it had been given to gaze upon the mystic Rose, upon that fairest Flower of Heaven, and who, in the fervour of his nascent faith, in the deep joy of his gratitude and love, was learning how sweet the Lord is!

But before entering upon this fresh retreat, which could be but an uninterrupted song of thanksgiving, there remained one duty to be discharged, one new happiness to be enjoyed. Having become the child of the Church, he yearned for the moment when he might be allowed to cast himself at the feet of the venerable Pontiff, who guides with so sure a hand, through the raging storm and wind, the bark which bears us all towards the heavenly haven.

We have heard the touching details o

this interview; and that we may make our readers partakers of our joy, we must seek an illustration from the most precious memories of Catholicism.

Those who have visited the catacombs will remember, that at every step they met the image of the Good Shepherd bearing back to the fold the wandering sheep; they will have remarked the expression of satisfied love, of fatherly tenderness, which the simple art of the first ages has rendered so truly. Let them now recall the feelings excited by this ever-recurring image, and then they may form some idea of this touching scene.

M. Ratisbonne and M. Théodore de Bussières were introduced to his Holiness by the reverend father the General of the Company of Jesus. After the customary genuflexions, they received that mighty benediction which Catholics prize so highly.

The holy Father conversed with them for some time, and gave them many precious tokens of his affection, with all the frank and tender love of a father. He gave directions that they should be taken to see the interior of his palace. Pushing them before him, with a gracious familiarity, he led them into his bedchamber. Then the venerable successor of the Prince of the Apostles gave them a touching evidence of his own trust in the protection of her whom the Church invokes as the Help of Christians; he showed them an image of the blessed Virgin which he reveres with an especial devotion, and which is placed close to his bed. And then, wishing that M. Ratisbonne should preserve some memorial of his visit, his Holiness gave him, with his own hands, a crucifix to which special indulgences were attached.

And if, when the days of trial and of conflict come, the new soldier of the faith shall need to refresh his courage, let him remember the sacred standard which the visible head of the Church then placed in his youthful hands; and, beholding his crucifix, let him say confidently, *In hoc signo vinces.*

Perhaps M. Ratisbonne will leave us before he has time to take root in this land of promise. It is so delightful to see one's family after a long absence, to embrace a brother who has preceded one in the way of the Lord. Far from weakening the heart's true ties, the Gospel sanctifies them and draws them closer; its most faithful disciples will ever be, in all that is not opposed to the law of God, the most tender of sons, the most devoted of friends.

If, then, Providence remove him too soon from our brotherly affection, let him go, like another apostle, fresh from the upper chamber, and manifest in his own country and in his father's house his new virtues, and exert the gentle constraint of his prayers, and diffuse the fragance and the grace of his youthful soul, which, born but yesterday into Catholic life, is still adorned with all the charms of infancy.

The earliest longings, the first thoughts of his heart, were for the regeneration of his brethren. Well, the Lord has read his secret heart, and has blessed him in regenerating that heart. In whatever way it may please God to lead him, our tender prayers will go with him, to draw down upon him the grace of perseverance; that the Author of every good and perfect gift may endue him with strength for the fight, with patience in the trial, with humility in the flush of victory, and a glowing charity.

Every young life is exposed to storm; happier than we are, he has been crowned before the conflict; but the evil days will come. May he then remember his brethren at **Rome!** May he never forget **Mary, his mother!**

BAPTISM OF M. MARIE-ALPHONSE RATISBONNE.

Extract from the letter of an eye-witness.

Paris, February 2d, 1842.

A FEW weeks since a stranger arrived in Rome. He was young and rich; he has all the habits of that elegance, all the tastes of that brilliant frivolity, which education and fortune impart to young men of his age and stamp. He asks nothing of Italy but to be lulled by the soft languors of her winters, and some rays of the sun of her antique glory, of the deathless splendour of her sky and of her summers, the ever-fresh charm of her old memories, and the fragance of poetry which exhales from her ruins, hallowed by great deeds and by great men.... In the secret heart of this young man there is one more serious thought, one profound and impetuous energy of feeling; he is a Jew, and he views Catholicism with all the prejudices and hatred of his race—with a hatred at once keen, implacable, and *sombre;* he even avoids Rome altogether. Still he has come thither, in his own despite almost; but he has scarcely arrived when he numbers the days for his departure. He has witnessed the moral degradation of his co-religionists, who are restrained to the filthiest quarter of the city—he charges it on the Catholics; and his hatred finds expression in bitter sarcasms, in horrible blasphemies. The very morning of the day fixed for his departure he wrote to his uncle: "I leave this city with a profound horror, and curse it as I go....." And that very day, a few hours later, this same young man casually enters a lonely church, falls on his knees overwhelmed and annihilated, rises bathed in tears, and asks for a Catholic priest, not to receive instruction, but to be baptised: his conversion was accomplished—he had *understood all*. What, then, had taken place in this church? What has he seen? what has he heard? I can tell you, for all Rome is vocal with it. But these are things belonging to an order so high and so holy, that it is the prerogative of the Church alone to utter them with the infallible warrant of her word. She will speak, and you will soon know all. So far as I am concerned, I will only relate to you to-day, without one touch of exaggeration, the facts of this conversion just as it happened, just as it struck me. It would be in itself an inexplicable miracle, even if a miracle had not been its efficient cause.

Mr. Alphonse Ratisbonne belongs to one of the chief Jewish families of Strasburg. Now, as if to accumulate moral impossibilities in the way of his conversion, God has permitted that its result should be obviously the ruin of his fairest hopes of fortune. and of the deepest affections of his heart. It severs the bonds of a love which has been already hallowed by solemn espousals. "A week since," he writes to his betrothed, "if any unforeseen calamity had compelled me to give you up, I could not have had the courage to do so; I should have died in the effort..... Now, to-day, if my new faith is to divide us, I shall offer this sacrifice to God without shedding one tear; and all my life long I shall pray that He may bless and enlighten you, and grant that we may meet in heaven."

Alphonse Ratisbonne made his public abjuration on the 31st of January, in the church of the Gesù, in presence of Cardinal Patrizi. The young catechumen, clothed in a long robe of white silk, was placed at the bottom of the church, below the barrier which separated him from the holy place, in compliance with the ancient custom preserved in our ritual. I did not then know him; but an undefinable interest, excited by the miraculous circumstances of his conversion, drew me towards him. I got as near to him as I could, rather to read upon his features the impressions of his soul, than to follow the touching ceremony of his abjuration. The cardinal, having prayed awhile at the altar, and assumed his pontifical vestments, went in procession towards the catechumen, at the bottom of the nave of the church. There commenced

the ceremonies and exorcisms. Never had I so felt the Divine character of that ritual, so full of mysteries. Can you conceive any thing more thrilling than this dialogue:
"What do you crave?"
"Baptism."
"What besides?"
"Life."
"Do you renounce the Devil?"
"I renounce him."
"Do you believe in Jesus Christ?"
"I do believe in him."
He, a descendant of those Jews who hanged Him on the wood of shame? All that is merely formal and outward had disappeared here. That firm, brief, energetic speech; that decided but modest look at the bishop who is questioning him; the noble firmness of his attitude, and the unruffled placidity of his features, the paleness of which was relieved by the faintest flush,—all these indications of a resolute, thoughtful, and collected character brought home to me the grandeur of this conflict, in which the rarest and most testing courage, that of a profound conviction without enthusiasm, without an enthralling imagination, had conquered that which is mightiest and most tenacious of life in the heart of man—his early faith and his first love. A sigh of ineffable happiness escaped from his breast; a smile, like a ray of heavenly beatitude, hovered around his lips, as

he raised his head, moist and dripping with the waters of Baptism. It was clear—every eye might see it—he had crossed a great gulf; he breathed, he was a Christian.

And then every barrier of the Church fell down before the innocence and the faith of this regenerated soul. Amidst the benedictions of the enormous crowd that filled the nave and just opened a pathway for him as he passed, the young neophyte was led to the altar. He there received the sacrament of Confirmation at the hands of the cardinal. As the gifts of the Holy Ghost descended, together with the blessing of the bishop, upon his head, he seemed to me oppressed beneath the torrent of grace; the waves of gladness that flowed in upon him were too vast—came too suddenly, too impetuously. It seemed as though, before opening his heart to the heavenly joys of his first communion, he needed time and rest to control his excess of holy emotion. The ceremony was suspended a while A voice, well known and dear to this pious congregation,—almost all French, or Catholic strangers, to whom the glorious popularity of our language was, like the faith, a common bond,—was heard celebrating the infinite mercies of God, and the wondrous patronage of Mary, manifested in the city of Rome towards a son of France. The Abbé Dupanloup's heart poured forth, spontaneously and without effort, a stream of lofty language, with the grace and masculine energy of a living faith, and with bursts of pathetic eloquence, to which his congregation could respond only by their tears.

At length the holy Sacrifice of the Mass began. I could not remove my eyes from M. Ratisbonne, absorbed entirely in his fulness of joy and in the fervour of his prayer. I fancied I could read upon his soul the growing impression of the bleeding memorials of Calvary. But I cannot express my meaning. And how shall I speak of this new pasch of this new Christian? How convey to you a notion of the solemn moment when the cardinal, tremulous with emotion, placed the sacred host upon his lips? At this last, highest grace, the vessel of election flowed over. He who had been, up to this moment, so calm in his fervour, so collected and firm, so entirely master of his deep feelings, could not now contain the fulness of this new and unknown bliss; he sobbed passionately, and was led almost fainting from the altar to his assigned place. And then was illustrated, in its sweetest symbol, the Catholic dogma of the communion of saints,—that mystery of universal and brotherly oneness, in virtue of which ten thousand times ten thousand of every tongue and of every land, who know not each other's names, meet and are one in the mystic feast, breaking together the bread of life everlasting, and drinking at one chalice the wine of boundless infinite charity. Noble ladies, girls in the first bloom of youth, young men, and men whose names and whose deeds are written in their country's annals, drew near with one accord to the holy table, offering to God for the new convert their fervent communions, just as mothers would have done for their children, or sisters for a brother, or friend for beloved friend. And the people, moved by this spectacle, joined their prayers and blessings by words, spoken loud—words of a simple sweetness and charm which cannot be transferred from their native Italian. At length the *Te Deum* thundered forth,—no other word can express the electrical effect of that exulting shout of thanksgiving, blending with the noble organ and the pealing bells of the Gesù. It is not a hymn of the Church, grave and measured, but rather the living acclaim of an enormous multitude swaying beneath an overmastering religious enthusiasm. I pray God that the memory of what I felt during those three hours may never be effaced from my heart; an impression like that is undoubtedly one of the most precious boons that can be bestowed upon a Christian soul.

THE CONVERSION OF

LETTER

OF

MARIE-ALPHONSE RATISBONNE

TO M. DUFRICHE-DESGENETTES,

Founder and Director of the "Archiconfrérie de Notre-Dame des Victoires," at Paris.

THIS letter was published in the first bulletin of the annals of the Archconfraternity. It was introduced by the curé of Notre-Dame des Victoires, with the following preface.

The news of the conversion of M. Alphonse Ratisbonne was communicated to the Archconfraternity of the Sacred Heart of Mary on Sunday, January 30th, 1842, at the evening service. It was brought by his brother, M. l'Abbé Théodore Ratisbonne, our sub-director. It would be impossible to describe the impression produced on all present by this touching and interesting narrative. When the Abbé Ratisbonne, after having recounted the circumstances of this wonderful conversion added, " This Alphonse, of whom I am speaking to you, is my brother..." the emotion of the congregation became most intense, and a prolonged murmur of wonder and of joy was heard throughout it. They had been marvelling at the Divine mercy, and rejoicing in the return of this prodigal to his father's house, with the common joy of Christians; but at the words, "he is my brother," all the congregation shared the rapture of the pious ecclesiastic, all felt that they too had gained a brother. At the request of many members of our confraternity, we sang the *Magnificat* in thanksgiving, just before I mounted the pulpit. For more than a year the family of the young neophyte had been the object of our eager desires and prayers, and, but a fortnight before his conversion, Alphonse had been again and specially commended by his brother to our public prayers.

As I wished to diffuse throughout the whole confraternity the sacred joy which filled our own hearts, and as I was anxious that my account should be scrupulously exact, I begged M. Marie-Alphonse Ratisbonne to be kind enough to give me, himself, a statement of the circumstances of his conversion; and I feel great pleasure in publishing the following extract from the letter he wrote in reply:

College of Juilly, 12th April, 1842.

My first thought and the first instinct of my heart, at the moment of my conversion, was to bury myself and my secret in the cloister, so that I might find refuge from the world, which could no longer understand me, and give myself entirely to my God, who had given me such a glimpse of the spiritual world. I was reluctant to speak without the permission of a priest. He, who was to me the representative and voice of God, commanded me to make known what had happened to me; and I did so, in so far as words enabled me to express my meaning. And now, after some weeks of retirement and retreat, I will try to set down a greater fulness of detail; and it is fitting that sinners should give an account of the graces vouchsafed to them to you, M. le Curé—to you who have founded the Archconfraternity for the conversion of sinners.

If I had only to apprise you of the fact of my conversion, one single word would suffice—the name of Mary. But your confraternity is eager to have a full account; you wish to know who and what is this son of Abraham, who has found at Rome life, and grace, and happiness. I will, therefore, first invoke the aid of my heavenly Mother, and then set before you, in very simple words, the course and order of my life.

My family is known well enough, for its members are rich and generous; and it has long occupied a high station in Alsace. It is said that my ancestors have been very godly men; Christians as well as Jews have blessed the name of my grandfather, the only Jew who obtained, under Louis XVI., not only the right to hold property at Strasburg, but a patent of nobility. Such was my family; but now all traditions of religion are effaced from it.

I began my studies at the Royal College of Strasburg, where I made far greater progress in the depravation of my heart than in the education of my mind.

It was in the year 1825 (I was born May 1st, 1814) that an unexpected event inflicted a heavy blow on my family. My brother Theodore, of whom the highest hopes were entertained, avowed himself a Christian; and soon after, nowithstanding the grief he had occasioned and the earnest entreaties of our parents, he became a priest, and exercised his ministry in the same city, and before the very eyes of my disconsolate family. Young as I was, my brother's conduct shocked me greatly, and I conceived a violent hatred of his office, and of his person and character. Brought up amongst young Christians, who were quite as reckless and indifferent as I was myself, I had not, up to that time, felt either sympathy or antipathy towards Christianity; but my brother's conversion, which I looked upon as an act of unaccountable folly, made me believe all I heard of the fanaticism of the Catholics, and I held them accordingly in great horror.

I was about this time, withdrawn from college to be placed in a Protestant institution, the magniloquent prospectus of which had dazzled my parents. The younger members of the great Protestant families of Alsace and of Germany came there, to be moulded upon the fashionable life of Paris, and abandoned themselves to pleasures of all kinds, far more than to study. Nevertheless, I presented myself for examination when I left this institution, and, by a piece of good luck I little deserved, I was admitted Bachelor of Arts.

I was then sole master of my patrimony; for my mother had died while I was still young, and my father had survived her but a few years. But I had a worthy uncle, the patriarch of the family, a second father to me, who, having no children of his own, had centred all his affection in those of his brother.

This uncle, so well known in the financial world for his lofty integrity as well as for his extraordinary capacity, wished much to give me a share in the bank of which he is the head; but I first of all read law at Paris, and, after having obtained the diploma of a licentiate and put on my advocate's gown, I was recalled to Strasburg by my uncle, who exerted all his influence to settle me with himself. I cannot number all his cares and kindnesses: horses, carriages, pleasant travels, a thousand acts of lavish affection, were mine, and he had not the heart to refuse me any thing. My uncle gave me a more positive mark of his confidence still: he gave me the signature of the bank, and he promised me besides the title and the solid advantages of a partner—a promise which he carried into effect the first of January in this year, 1842. I was at Rome when this information reached me.

My uncle had only one matter of complaint.—my frequent journeys to Paris. You are too fond of the *Champs-Élysées*, said he affectionately to me. He was right. I loved nothing but pleasures; business annoyed me, the atmosphere of the office stifled me; I had a notion that people came into the world simply to enjoy themselves; and, although a kind of natural and instinctive modesty kept me from baser pleasures and associates, I thought of nothing but fêtes and rejoicings, and gave myself up to them with passionate ardour.

It was fortunate that about this time a good work offered itself to my eager need of action, and I threw myself into it with all my heart. It was the work of the *regeneration* of the poor Israelites, as it was erroneously called; for I have now learned that something more than money and lotteries of charity is requisite to regenerate a people destitute of religion. But I honestly believed in the possibility of this renovation, and I became one of the most zealous members of the Society for the providing occupation for young Jews,—a society which my brother had founded at Strasburg fifteen years before, and which has lasted until now, notwithstanding its limited resources. I managed to fill its coffers, and fancied I had done something very great.

O Christian charity, how thou wouldst smile at my lofty self-satisfaction! The Jew thinks a great deal of himself when he has given a great deal; the Christian gives all and despises himself—he despises himself until he has given himself in addition; and when he has sacrified himself whole and entire, he despises himself still.

Although I had no religion whatever, I was busy with the worldly condition of my *co-religionists*. I was a Jew by profession. and that is all; for I did not even believe in God. I never opened a religious book; and neither in my uncle's house nor in those of my brothers and sisters was there the slightest observance of the injunctions of Judaism.

There was a fearful void in my heart, and I was not happy, though I possessed every thing in abundance, in profusion. Something was still lacking; and this something I found, at least so I fondly fancied; and it was thus:

I had a niece, the daughter of my eldest brother, who had been destined to me from our childhood. She was growing up, under my own eyes, in beauty and in gracefulness, and in her I beheld the fair promise of my future life, and the satisfaction of all my hopes. I do not think it seemly to set forth here the praises of her who was my betrothed. It would be useless to those who do not know her; but those who have seen her know that it would not be easy to imagine a young girl more gentle, more amiable, more charming. She was to me a creature apart, who seemed formed expressly to complete my existence; and when the desires of all our family, combined with our mutual symathy and affection, fixed the time of my long-wished-for marriage, I thought that nothing could be thenceforth wanting to my happiness.

And thus, after the ceremony of our betrothal, I had the pleasure of seeing all my family overflowing with joy, and my sisters so happy! They had but one reproach to make—I loved my bride too exclusively, and they confessed their jealousy; for I may say in passing, that there are few families so happy as mine: the most intimate and perfect union of hearts, the most tender affection, reigns amongst my brothers and sisters—an affection which verged on idolatry. . . . And, indeed, my sisters are so good, so loving, and so lovely. . . . Why, alas, are they not Christians?

There was only one member of our family who was hateful to me—my brother Theodore. And yet he loved us well; but his *soutane* repelled me, his presence oppressed me with gloom, his grave and serious conversation excited my wrath. About a year before my betrothal I had found it impossible to restrain my feelings, and I expressed them to him in a letter, which was intended to sever all connection between us for ever. The occasion was this. A child was lying in the agony of death; my brother Theodore had the assurance to ask permission to baptise it, and he would probably have succeeded, if I had not been informed of his intention. I looked on it as an unworthy and dishonourable attempt; I wrote to the *priest* to try his strength with men and not with children; and I accompanied these words with so many invectives and threatenings, that I am even now astonished that my brother did not answer me a single word. He continued his relations with the rest of the family; but I would never see him again, and I cherished a blind and bitter hatred against priests, and churches, and convents, and especially against the Jesuits, whose very name goaded me to frenzy.

Fortunately my brother left Strasburg, and so gratified my most earnest wish. He was summoned to Paris, to Notre Dame des Victoires, where, he said as he bade us farewell, he should not cease to pray for the conversion of his brothers and sisters. His departure relieved me of a heavy weight; I even yielded so far to the entreaties of my family as to write him a few words of apology on the occasion of my betrothal. He answered my letter affectionately, and commended to my care some few poor people in whom he felt interested; and I gave them some trifling sum.

After this sort of reconciliation I had no further connection with Theodore, and I had altogether ceased to think of him; I had forgotten him quite. . . and he, the while, was praying for me!

I ought to mention here a kind of revolution in my religious notions which took place about the time of the ceremony of my betrothal. As I have said, I believed in nothing; and in this complete nullity, this negation of all faith, I found myself perfectly in harmony with my young friends, whether Catholic or Protestant. But the look of my bride awakened within me a mysterious sense of human dignity and worth; I began to believe in the immortality of the soul; more than that, I began, by a kind of instinct, to pray to God; I thanked Him for my happiness: and for all that I was not happy. . . I could not analyse and account for my feelings; I looked on my sweet bride as my good angel; I often told her so; and, indeed, the thought of her raised my heart towards a God whom I knew not, whom I had never before invoked.

It was deemed right, by reason of the tender age of my bride, to postpone our marriage. She was only sixteen years old I was to undertake a voyage of pleasure to beguile the time of expectation. I scarcely knew whither to direct my wanderings; one of my sisters, who is settled in Paris, wished me to remain with her; a dear friend wanted to take me off to Spain. I declined the invitations of some others, who made me very attractive propositions. I resolved, at length, to go straight to Naples, to pass the winter at Malta for the benefit of my rather delicate health, and then to return home by way of the East. I got letters of introduction for Constantinople even; and I set out about the end of November, 1841, intending to return in the spring of 1842.

My leave-taking was very melancholy. I left behind me my beloved bride, an uncle whose whole affection rested on me, sisters, brothers, nieces, whose society was my most valued delight; I left also those industrial schools, those poor Jews with whom I was so actively employed, and the numerous friends who loved me—friends of my childhood, whom I could not leave without shedding tears; for indeed I loved them, and love them still. . . .

To set out alone on so long a voyage! the mere thought threw me into a state of profound sadness. But, said I to myself, perhaps God will send me some friend on my way!

I recollect two singular incidents which marked the days preceding my departure, and which now strike me forcibly. I wished before leaving, to affix my signature to a large number of receipts connected with the subscriptions to the Jewish industrial society . . . . . I dated them in advance January 15th, and by dint of writing this date so many times, I became weary of it, and said, as I laid down my pen:

"God only knows where I shall be on the 15th of January, and whether that day may not be the day of my death."

On that day I arrived at Rome, and I regard it as the first dawn of my new life.

Another circumstance that interested me was the meeting of several distinguished Jews to consider the means of reforming the worship of Judaism, and bringing it more into harmony with the spirit of the age. I went to the meeting, at which every one gave his opinion on the improvements that were suggested. There were as many opinions as persons; there was a great deal of discussion; they took into account the convenience of man, the events of the times, the axioms of public opinion, all the ideas of modern civilisation: every thing was thought of and pondered, one only was forgotten—the law of God. That did not seem to come into the question at all; I cannot remember that the name of God was mentioned once, or that of Moses, or the existence of the Bible.

My own private opinion was, that they should allow all religious forms to die quietly out; that they need not have recourse either to books or to men, but that every one should be left free to express and practise his faith in his own fashion. This opinion proves my lofty wisdom in matters of religion. I had made progress as you will see. The meeting broke up without coming to any decision.

But a Jew, more sensible than I, had given utterance to a sentiment so remarkable, that I will give it word for word: "We must make haste to abandon this old temple, whose crumbling walls are parting on all sides, unless we wish to be buried beneath its ruins;" words full of truth, words which every Jew of our times murmurs to himself alone. But, alas, eighteen centuries have passed since they abandoned their ancient temple, and they will not enter that new temple whose gates are open to them by day and by night!

At length I set out. As I left Strasburg I shed many tears; I was disquieted by a crowd of fears, by a thousand strange presentiments. When we stopped to change horses, I was roused from my reverie by cries of joy and the sound of music. It was a rustic wedding—the happy, noisy villagers were just issuing from the church—flutes and fiddles were going vigorously; the crowd came round my carriage, as though to invite me to share their joy. "It will be my turn soon," I exclaimed. And this thought restored my cheerfulness.

I spent some days at Marseilles. where my friends and relatives received me with open arms. I could scarcely tear myself from all this elegant hospitality. And truly it needs an effort to leave France, when one leaves also a whole life of love, and of loving memories and associations. Besides the ties which bound me to her shores, the sea itself seemed to oppose my departure; it rolled along its mighty waves to bar my progress; but all these obstacles were swept away by the steamer which took me to Naples. I was soon able to enjoy the magnificent type of infinity above me and around me; but what struck me more than sea or sky was *man*, that frail creature who braves all dangers, and masters the elements themselves. My pride was loftier than the rolling waves, more tenacious of its aims, and far less easily subjugated.

The boat touched at Civita Vecchia on its way to Naples. As we entered the harbour the sound of cannon greeted our ears. I asked, with a spiteful curiosity, the motive of this warlike sound on the peaceful territory of the Pope. I received for answer, "It is the feast of the Conception of Mary." I shrugged my shoulders and would not land.

The next day we reached Naples. The sun was shining gloriously, and producing brilliant effects on the smoke of Vesuvius. Never had I been so dazzled by any scene of nature. I saw before me the reality of those glowing images of the heavens and the sea with which artists and poets had stored my fancy.

I passed a month at Naples, that I might see and describe every thing. I wrote bitter things against the religion and the priests, who seemed to me so out of keeping with that magnificent country. Oh, with what blasphemies did I fill my journal! And if I speak of them now, it is that you may see how dark and evil was my soul then. I wrote to Strasburg that I had drunk some *lachryma Christi* on Vesuvius to the health of the abbé Ratisbonne, and that tears like that did me good too. I cannot transcribe the horrible witticisms that I permitted myself to write.

My betrothed asked me if I agreed with those who said: "See Naples and die." No, I replied; but see Naples and live; live to see it again. Such was my state of mind.

I had no wish to go to Rome, although two friends of my family, whom I saw frequently, urged me strongly to do so; I mean M. Coulman, a Protestant, and formerly *député* of Strasburg, and Baron Rothschild, whose family lavished on me every kind of attention and of gratification. I could not yield to their persuasions..... My betrothed wished me to go direct to Malta; and she sent me a recommendation from my physician that I should spend the winter there, and carefully avoid Rome, because of the malignant fevers which, he said, prevailed there.

These reasons would have prevented my going to Rome, even if I had placed this journey on my original programme. I thought I might possibly go there on my return, and I took my place in the *Mongibello* for Sicily. A friend accompanied me on board of the vessel, and promised to return and bid me farewell before we started. He came, but did not find me. If M. de Rèchecourt should ever learn the reason of my breach of engagement, he will be able to account for my apparent incivility, and will, I am sure, forgive me.

M. Coulman had introduced me to an amiable and estimable man who was going to Malta. I was so pleased at this, that I said to myself: "This is surely the friend God has sent me."

However, the first day of the new year arrived, and the vessel had not left. It was a sad day to me. I was alone at Naples; no one to congratulate me and wish me well, no one to press to my heart. I thought of my family, of the festivity and joy with which my uncle always kept that day; I began to shed tears, and the lively gaiety of the Neapolitans deepened my sadness. I went out, to shake off my importunate melancholy, and followed mechanically in the train of the crowd. I reached the *place* in front of the palace, and found myself, I know not how, at the door of a church. I went in. I think a priest was saying Mass. I remained there, leaning against a pillar, and my heart seemed to open and expand in a new atmosphere. I prayed after my own fashion, without taking any notice of what was going on around me; I prayed for my betrothed, for my uncle, for my deceased father, for the loving mother who had been taken from me so early, for all who were dear to me; and I asked of God some inspiration, some intimation of His will which might guide me in my projects for improving the condition of the Jews,— projects which haunted me incessantly.

My sadness passed away, like a cloud which the wind breaks up and disperses; and my heart was filled with an unutterable calmness, with a consolation such as I should have felt if a voice had said to me: " Your prayer is heard." Yes, it was heard,—heard far beyond all expectation; for on the last day of that same month I was to be baptised in a church at Rome!

But how did I get to Rome?

I do not know, nor can I account for it in any way. I almost fancy I must have missed my way; for instead of going to the *bureau* of the Palermo boats, as I intended when I left my lodging, I found myself in that of the diligences for Rome. I told M. Vigne, the friend who was to accompany me to

Malta, that I could not resist the temptation of making a short expedition to Rome, but that I would certainly be at Naples so as to leave with him on the 20th of January. I was wrong to pledge myself thus; for God disposes; and that 20th of January was destined to mark a very different crisis in my life. I left Naples on the 5th, and reached Rome on the 6th, the feast of the Epiphany. I had for my fellow-traveller an Englishman, named Marshall, whose original conversation amused me much.

Rome did not at first produce on me the impression I had expected. And I was so pressed for time, that I eagerly devoured ruins, ancient and modern, with the avidity of a thorough tourist. I filled my imagination and my journal with a confused medley of reminiscences. I visited with a monotonous admiration galleries, churches, catacombs, and all the innumerable magnificences of Rome. I was most frequently accompanied by my English friend, and by a *valet de place;* I have no notion what religion they were of, for neither of them gave any sign of Christianity in the churches, and I believed I behaved far more reverently than they did.

On the 8th of January, as I was going my round of sight-seeing, I heard some one calling me in the street; it was my old friend Gustave de Bussières. I was very happy to meet him, for my isolation had become painful to me. We went to dine with my friend's father; and in that agreeable circle I felt some measure of the joy with which one greets any memorial of one's own country in a strange land.

As I entered the drawing-room, M. Théodore de Bussières, the eldest son of this honourable family, was leaving it. I did not know him personally, but I knew that he was my brother's friend and namesake; I knew that he had deserted Protestantism and become a Catholic, and this was quite enough to inspire me with a profound antipathy to him. I fancied that this feeling was reciprocal. However, as M. Théodore de Bussières was already well known by his published volume of travels in Sicily and in the East, I was very glad to ask him some questions before starting on the same track; and whether on this account, or from mere civility, I signified my intention of paying him a visit. He answered me very kindly, and added, that he had just received a letter from my brother the abbé, and that he would give me his new address. "I will gladly receive it," said I, "although I shall not need it."

There our conversation ended; and when he had left, I felt annoyed at the obligation I had imposed on myself to make a useless visit and waste my very precious time.

I continued running about Rome all day long except two hours in the morning which

I spent with Gustave; and in the evening I took my ease, either at the theatre or at some party. My conversations with Gustave were very animated; for the intercourse of two old schoolfellows furnishes inexhaustible store of amusing and interesting souvenirs. But he was a Protestant, with all the zeal and enthusiasm of the pietists of Alsace. He talked largely of the superiority of his sect to all other Christian communities, and was very eager to convert me; and I was much amused, as I had fancied that the mania of proselytism was peculiar to Catholics. I generally evaded his assaults by some merry jest; but once, to console him for the failure of his attempts, I promised him, that if ever I took it into my head to be converted, I would turn pietist; and he, on his part, promised that he would be present at my marriage, in the August following. All his efforts to detain me at Rome were ineffectual. Others of my friends, M. Edmund Humann and Alfred de Lotzbeck, joined with him in begging me to remain in Rome for the Carnival. But I could not consent; I feared I should grieve and distress my betrothed, and M. Vigne expected me at Naples in time to start with him on the 20th of January.

I was making the best use of the short time that remained, and went to the Capitol to visit the church of Aracœli. The imposing appearance of this church, the solemn chants which were echoing along its vast nave, the historical recollections awakened in me by the very soil I was treading,—all combined to produce a profound impression upon me. I was moved, penetrated, transported; and my *valet de place*, noticing my emotion, told me that he had frequently seen strangers affected in a similar way in that church.

As we came down from the Capitol, my *cicerone* led me through the Ghetto, the quarter assigned to the Jews. There I felt an emotion of an entirely different kind— mingled pity and indignation. What, I exclaimed, as I beheld that miserable sight, is this that Roman charity of which so much is said? I shuddered with horror, and I asked myself whether a whole nation deserved to be the victims of such barbarous treatment and of such endless prejudices, simply for having killed one man eighteen hundred years ago! Alas, I knew not then who this *One Man* was—I knew not the cry of blood which this people had uttered —a cry which I dare not repeat here, and which I cannot bear to recall. Rather would I dwell upon that other cry, wafted to heaven from the cross, *Father, forgive them; for they know not what they do!*

I described all that I had seen and felt to my family. I remember having written, that I preferred being of the number of the oppressed to being in the camp of the oppressors. I went back again to the Capitol, and found the church of Aracœli in a great bustle of preparation for some grand ceremony. I asked the object of it, and was told that two Jews, named Constantini, of Ancona, were going to be baptised. I cannot describe the indignation I felt on receiving this information; and when my guide asked me if I should like to be present I exclaimed: " What! *I* assist at so infamous a spectacle! No, no; I should not be able to restrain myself from making a desperate onslaught on both priests and victims."

I may say, without exaggeration, that I never felt so fierce a hatred towards Christianity as after that visit to the Ghetto. The stream of my mockery and blasphemy flowed incessantly and inexhaustibly.

However, I had a few farewell visits to make, and my promise to Baron de Bussières occurred to me continually as an awkward obligation gratuitously taken on myself. Most fortunately I had not asked his address, and I resolved to make this circumstance my excuse for not performing my promise.

It was now the 15th, and I went to take my place for Naples; my departure was fixed for the 17th, at three A.M. I had two days left, and I employed them, as usual, in running about. But, as I was coming out of a book-shop in which I had been looking over some works on Constantinople, I met a servant of M. de Bussières senior, on the *Corso*. He saluted me in passing, and I stopped him to ask the address of M. Théodore de Bussières: he replied, with an Alsatian accent: Piazza Nicosia, No. 38.

And now, whether I liked it or not, I was committed to this visit. I put it off to the last moment, and at length set off, carrying in my hand a card on which I had written *p. p. c.* I found out this Piazza Nicosia, after a great many turns and windings, and at 'ength reached No. 38. It was the very next door to the bureau at which I had taken my place for Naples the same day. I had made a good round to reach the point from which I had started—type of many a journey of life on earth! But from that point I set forth on a journey of which I little thought!

My reception at the house of M. de Bussières was annoying. Instead of simply taking my card, the servant suddenly announced me, and introduced me into the drawing-room. I concealed my vexation as well as I could beneath a civil smile, and I took a chair near Madame de Bussières, who was sitting with her two daughters, graceful and gentle as the angels that Raphael painted. Our conversation was at first very general and unmeaning; but it soon began to take the tone and hue of the deep passion with which I related my impressions of Rome.

I looked on M. de Bussières as a *dévot*, in the illnatured sense of the word, and I was very glad to have the opportunity of teasing him about the Jews of Rome. It was a relief to me to do so; but my complaints of course led our conversation upon religious ground. M. de Bussières spoke to me of the majesty and grandeur of Catholicism; and I replied with irony, and some of the many imputations I had either heard or read; but I could not help checking my impious frenzy, out of respect for Madame de Bussières and the two dear children who were playing at her side. "Well," said M. de Bussières, "since you detest superstition, and profess yourself so very liberal in point of doctrine —since you are so enlightened an *esprit fort* —have you the courage to submit yourself to a very simple and innocent test?"

"What test?"

"Only to wear a little something I will give you; look, it is a medal of the Blessed Virgin. It seems very ridiculous, does it not? But, I assure you, I attach great value and efficacy to this little medal."

This proposal, I confess, astonished me by its puerile oddity. I did not expect such a bathos. My first impulse was to laugh and shrug my shoulders; but it struck me that this scene could furnish me a delicious chapter for my journal; and I consented to take the medal, that I might give it to my betrothed as a confirmation of my story. No sooner said than done. The medal was passed round my neck, not without difficulty, however, for the ribbon was rather too short. At length we succeeded; I had the medal on my heart, and I exclaimed with a hearty laugh, "Ha, ha, here I am, a Catholic, apostolic and Roman!"

It was the devil prophesying by my mouth.

M. de Bussières felt a childlike pleasure in his victory, and was eager to grasp all its advantages. "Now," said he, "you must perfect the test; you must say every night and morning the *Memorare*, a very short and very efficacious prayer which S. Bernard addressed to the Blessed Virgin Mary."

"What do you mean, with your *Memorare?*" I exclaimed; "come, let us have done with this folly."

The name of S. Bernard reminded me of my brother, who had written the life of this great saint. I had never read his book; and this association kindled afresh all my antipathy to proselytism, Jesuitism, and all those whom I called hypocrites and apostates.

I begged M. de Bussières to drop the subject; and I said, with a smile of contempt, that I regretted my not having a Hebrew prayer to offer him in return: but I had not one, and could not recollect one.

However, he persisted; he said that by refusing to recite this short prayer I made the test useless, and that I proved thereby the reality of the wilful obstinacy with which the Jews were reproached. I did not wish to attach too much importance to the matter, and so I said: "Well, then, I promise you to say this prayer. Anyhow, if it does me no good, it cannot do me any harm." And M. de Bussières went to look for it, and gave it to me, begging me to copy it for him. I consented, on condition that I might keep the original, and give him my copy. I had no other thought than to enrich my journal with this additional *pièce justificative*.

And now we were both satisfied. Our conversation seemed to me whimsical and very amusing. I took my departure, and spent the evening at the theatre, thinking no more either of my medal or of the *Memorare*. But when I came home I found a note from M. de Bussières, who had called to return my visit, begging me to see him once more before I left Rome. I had to return his *Memorare;* and as I was to leave in the morning, I packed my trunks and made all my preparations, and then I sat down and copied the prayer, *Memorare, O piissima Virgo.* . . . I wrote these words of S. Bernard mechanically, without thinking of their meaning. I was very tired; it was very late, and I needed rest.

The next day, the 16th of January, I got my passport signed, and completed all my preparations; but as I walked along I could not help repeating the words of the *Memorare*. Whence was it, O my God, that these words had taken so firm, so deep hold on my mind? I could not put them away; they returned importunately upon me. I said them over and over again, just as one hums a tune which haunts one involuntarily and without conscious effort.

About eleven o'clock I called on M. de Bussières, to return to him his tenacious and peremptory prayer. I talked to him about my proposed travels in the East, and he gave me much excellent advice. "But," said he suddenly, "it is strange that you persist in leaving Rome at the very time when people are coming from all parts for the great ceremonies at St. Peter's. Perhaps you may never have the chance again; and you will be sorry to have lost an opportunity which so many seek with eager curiosity."

I replied that my place was taken and paid for; that I had written to inform my family of my departure; that I expected letters at Palermo; that it was now too late to think of changing my plans, and that my mind was made up. Our conversation was interrupted by the postman, who brought a letter from my brother, the Abbé Ratisbonne. He showed me the letter; but it was quite devoid of interest to me, as it related to a work which M. de Bussières was publishing in Paris. My brother did not even know that I was in Rome; but this unexpected episode threatened to close my visit, as I was eager to avoid every thing that could remind me of my brother.

Nevertheless, I was induced, by some incomprehensible influence, to prolong my stay at Rome. I granted to the urgency of a man whom I scarcely knew, what I had obstinately refused to my most intimate friends and companions.

And what, O my God, what was that irresistible impulse which led me to do what I had so firmly resolved not to do? Was it not a continuation of the same sweet force which brought me from Strasburg to Italy, notwithstanding my tempting invitations to Paris and to Valencia?—which led me from Naples to Rome, in spite of my firm determination to go straight to Sicily?—which at Rome compelled me, on the eve of my departure, to pay a visit which annoyed me, while I neglected others which I should have liked? O wonderful leadings of Providence? There is a mysterious influence which goes with us all along the course of our life. I had received the name of Tobias together with that of Alphonse. I had quite forgotten my name; but the unseen angel had not forgotten me; he was the true and helpful friend whom God had sent me—but I knew him not Alas, how many are there in the world who know not the celestial guide of their journey and who resist his gentle voice!

I had no wish to spend the Carnival in Rome, but I did wish to see the Pope; and M. de Bussières had assured me that I should see him very soon at St. Peter's. We took several rambles together. We talked over every thing we saw—monuments, pictures, manners and customs; but religion contrived to mix itself with every thing. M. de Bussières introduced it with such charming simplicity, enforced it with so keen and ardent a zeal, that I often said to myself, that if any thing could disgust a man with religion, it was the very importunity with which his conversion was sought. My natural gaiety led me to turn the most serious subjects into ridicule, and the light flashes of my fancy too often deepened into the fiendish glare of blasphemy. Even now I shudder at thought of those days.

And yet M. de Bussières was uniformly calm and indulgent, even though he could not conceal his grief. He even said once: "In spite of your rage, I have a sure conviction that you will be a Christian one day; for there is in you a groundwork of rectitude which comforts me when I think of you, and persuades me that you will be enlightened, even though an angel from heaven be needed for that end."

"Ha, well and good," said I; "for else the matter would not be easy to manage."

As we passed the *Scala Santa*, M. de Bussères was seized with a fit of enthusiasm. He rose up in the carriage, uncovered his head, and said in a tone of fervour: "Hail, *Scala Santa!* here is a sinner who will one day mount you on his knees!"

It would be utterly impossible to express the effect produced on me by this unexpected movement, this extraordinary honour paid to some old steps. I laughed at it as at something hopelessly, grotesquely mad; and as, a short time after, we drove through the charming gardens of the Villa Wolkonski, I rose and parodied his apostrophe by saying: "Hail, true marvels of God's power! It is before you that I kneel in homage, and not before an old staircase!"

These drives were repeated on the two following days, and lasted about two hours each. On the 19th, I saw M. de Bussières again, but he seemed sad and dejected. I withdrew from a motive of delicacy, without inquiring the cause of his sadness. Indeed, I did not learn this until the next day at noon, in the church of S. Andrea delle Fratte.

I was to leave on the 22d of January; for I had a second time taken my place for Naples. The engagements of M. de Bussières seemed to have diminished his zeal for my conversion, and I fancied he had forgotten all about his miraculous medal; but still I kept on muttering to myself, though with an inconceivable impatience, that everlasting importunate invocation of St. Bernard.

In the middle of the night before the 20th of January, I awoke suddenly, and saw before me a large black cross, of a peculiar form, and without the figure of our Lord. I made many attempts to get rid of this image, but I could not succeed; however I turned, there it was always before me. I cannot say how long this lasted, for I fell asleep at length; and when I awoke in the morning I thought no more of it.

I had to write several letters, and I remember that one of them, written to the younger sister of my betrothed, ended with the words, "*que Dieu vous garde*,"—may God protect you! Some little time after I received a letter from my bride, dated that same 20th of January, and ending with the same words, "*que Dieu vous garde!*" And, indeed, that day was under the especial care and guardianship of God.

Yet, if any one had said to me that morning, "You have risen a Jew; you will lie down a Christian,..." I should have looked on him as hopelessly, ludicrously mad.

This Thursday, January 20th, after having

taken breakfast at my hotel, and carried my letters to the post, I went to call on my friend Gustave, the pietist, who had just returned from a shooting excursion which had taken him for some days from Rome. He was surprised to see me still in Rome; I told him my motive for remaining was to see the Pope. "But I shall leave without seeing him after all, I said; for he took no part in the ceremony of the *Cathedra Petri*, although I had been led to hope he would do so."

Gustave consoled me ironically by speaking of another ceremony, and a very curious one, he said, which was to take place, I think, at S. Maria Maggiore. He alluded to the blessing of the animals; and thereupon followed a shower of jests and sarcasms, just such as you can imagine a Jew and a Protestant would utter.

We parted about eleven o'clock, after making an appointment for the next day to see a picture which had been painted for our countryman, Baron de Lotzbeck. I went off to a *café* in the Piazza di Spagna to look at the newspapers; and I had scarcely entered it when M. Edmond Humann sat down at my side, and we talked very gaily about Paris, and the fine arts and politics. Soon another friend accosted me; he was a Protestant, M. Alfred de Lotzbeck, with whom I held a conversation more frivolous still. We talked of hunting, of all kinds of pleasures, of the mirth of the Carnival, of the brilliant *soirée* given the evening before by the Duke de Torlonia. Nor did we forget the fêtes of my approaching marriage, to which I invited M. de Lotzbeck, who promised faithfully to be present.

If at that moment—it was noon—a third person had come up to me, and had said, "Alphonse, in a quarter of an hour you will be adoring Jesus Christ, your God and your Saviour; you will be prostrate in a poor church; you will be smiting your breast at the feet of a priest in a convent of Jesuits, where you will spend the Carnival in preparing for your baptism; and you will feel ready to offer yourself in sacrifice for the Catholic faith; you will renounce the world, its pomps, its pleasures; your fortune, your hopes, your bright glad future; and if necessary, you will renounce your betrothed also, and the love of your family, the esteem of your friends, the attachment of the Jews;... and you will have but one aspiration, to follow Jesus Christ, and to bear His cross even unto death;..."—I say that if some prophet had uttered before me a prediction like this, I should have thought that there could be only one man more mad than he, the man who could believe in the possibility of any thing so absurd. And yet it is this absurdity and folly which compose now my wisdom and **my** happiness.

As I left the *café*, I met the carriage of M. Théodore de Bussières. He stopped, and asked me to go with him for a drive. The weather was magnificent, and I accepted his invitation with pleasure. But M. de Bussières asked my permission to stop a few minutes at the church of S. Andrea delle Fratte, which was close by, as he had some little business there. He asked me to wait for him in the carriage; but I preferred getting out to look round the little church. They were busy with preparations for a funeral, and I inquired the name of the deceased person for whom these honours were intended. M. de Bussières replied, "It is one of my friends, Count de Laferronnays; his sudden death is the cause of the depression of spirits you may have observed in me the last day or two."

I did not know M. de Laferronnays, I had never even seen him; and so I felt nothing more than that vague kind of sorrow which one always feels at hearing of a sudden death. M. de Bussières left me to make some arrangements about the tribune that was to be set apart for the family of the deceased. "I shall not tax your patience long," said he; "I shall not be away more than a few minutes."

The church of S. Andrea delle Fratte is small, poor, and almost deserted; I think I was almost the only person in it, and there was no work of art to attract my attention.

I was looking round mechanically, without any definite thought or purpose; I remember only a black dog, which bounded and jumped before me as I moved about.... Suddenly the dog disappeared, the whole church disappeared; I saw nothing further,... or rather, O my God, I saw one only object!

And how should I speak of it? Ah, no, no words of man can even attempt to utter the unutterable; all description, how sublime soever, must of necessity be only a degradation of the ineffable reality.

I lay there, prostrate, bathed in tears, my heart completely absorbed and lost, when M. de Bussières recalled me to life. I could not answer his eager hurried questions; but at length I grasped the medal which I wore in my bosom; I kissed with fervent emotion the image of the Virgin, radiant with grace. Oh, yes, it was indeed her very self!

I knew not where I was; I knew not whether I was Alphonse Ratisbonne or not; I was so entirely changed, that I did not know myself.... I seemed to seek to identify myself, and to fail in the effort;... the most glowing joy pervaded my heart; I could not speak, I could reveal nothing; I felt within me something so awful and so sacred, that I asked for a priest.... I was taken to one, and it was only at his positive command that I spoke as well as I could, on my knees, and with a palpitating heart.

My first utterance was an expression of gratitude to M. de Laferronnays and to the Archconfraternity of Notre-Dame des Victoires. I knew intuitively that M. de Laferronnays had prayed for me.* I cannot tell how I knew it, any more than I can account for the truths of which I had suddenly gained both the knowledge and the belief. All I can say is, that the moment when the Blessed Virgin made a sign with her hand, the veil fell from my eyes; not one veil only, but all the veils which were wrapped around me disappeared, just as snow melts beneath the rays of the sun.

I came forth from a tomb, from an abyss of darkness; and I was living, perfectly, energetically living.... and yet I shed tears. I saw before me the fearful miseries from which I had been rescued by the mercy of God; I shuddered at the sight of my innumerable sins, and I was stupefied, melted, almost crushed by a sense of wonder and of gratitude.... I thought of my brother with a joy beyond words; but tears of compassion were

---

* M. de Laferronnays died suddenly on the evening of the 17th of January, 1842, after a life of edifying and consistent piety. The day before he had dined at Prince Borghese's, and M de Bussières had commended the young Jew, in whom he felt so much interested, to his prayers. M. de Laferronnays manifested a singular interest in this conversion.

mingled with my tears of love. Alas, that so many should go quietly down into this yawning abyss with their eyes closed by pride or by indifference... should go down and be swallowed up of this horrible darkness... and then, my family, my betrothed, my poor sisters! O torturing anxiety! My thoughts were of you, O ye beloved ones,—my first prayers were for you!... And are you never to raise your eyes towards the Saviour of the world, whose blood hath blotted out original sin? O, how foul is the blot of that stain! how completely it obliterates every trace by which we might recognise the creature that was made in the image of God!

I am asked how I attained a knowledge of these truths, since it is well known that I never opened a religious book, had never read a page of the Bible, and that the dogma of original sin, which is either denied or utterly forgotten by the modern Jews, had never for a single moment occupied my thoughts,—indeed, I doubt whether I had ever heard the words which express it. How, then, did I arrive at a knowledge of it? I know not. All that I know is, that when I entered that church I was profoundly ignorant of every thing, and that when I came out I saw every thing clearly and distinctly. The only explanation I can suggest is, that I was like a man suddenly roused from slumber, or rather, like a man born blind, whose eyes are suddenly opened;—he sees indeed, but he can give no definition of that light which enlightens him, and in which he beholds the objects of his wondering gaze. And if we cannot explain the light of nature, how should we be able to explain that light which is in reality the very truth itself? I think I state the precise truth when I say that I knew not *the letter*, but that I grasped fully the inner meaning and the spirit of the Catholic dogmas. I rather *felt* than *saw* them; and I felt them by the indescribable effects they produced within me. The scene of these wonders was within, in my soul; and their impressions, ten thousand times more swift than thought, ten thousand times deeper than reflection, had not only shaken my soul to its foundation, but had, as it were, turned it round, and given it another direction, towards another end, and in the power of a new life.

I know I am expressing my meaning very badly: but can you expect, monsieur, that I should be able to measure with narrow and dry speech those emotions which my heart itself could with difficulty contain?

But however inexact and imperfect these my words may be, the simple fact of the case is, that I found myself in some sort like a bare and naked being; my soul was a *tabula rasa*. . . . The world had no longer any existence for me; my prejudices against Christianity were no more; the instincts and prepossessions of my childhood were gone, and had left no trace; the love of my God had so entirely ejected and replaced every other love, that my betrothed herself appeared to me in quite another light: I loved her as one might love any object which God held within His outstretched hands, as a precious gift which yet more endears the giver.

I repeat that I implored my confessor, Father Villefort, and M. de Bussières to observe an inviolable secrecy in regard of what had happened to me. My earnest wish was to bury myself in a Trappist monastery, and occupy myself exclusively with the things of eternity; and, besides, I confess I thought that my family and my friends would deem me crazed—that they would turn me into ridicule; and that it was better for me in every way to escape entirely from the world —from its opinions and its judgments.

However, my ecclesiastical superiors showed me that this ridicule, reproach, and false judgments were but a part of that chalice which is put to the lips of every real Christian; they urged me not to decline this chalice, and told me how Jesus Christ had predicted to His disciples, sufferings, torments, and anguish. These solemn and pregnant word were, so far from discouraging me, that they increased my interior joy; I felt myself ready and prepared for every thing, and I eagerly craved baptism. They wished to interpose some delay: "but," I exclaimed, "those Jews who heard the preaching of the Apostles were baptised immediately, and you wish to put me off, after I have heard the Queen of Apostles!" My deep emotion, my vehement desire, my repeated supplications touched the hearts of these holy men; and I was consoled by the blessed promise of an early baptism.

I could scarcely await the day fixed upon for the fulfilment of this promise, so foul and deformed I felt myself before God; and yet, what kindness, what love was lavished on me during those days of my preparation! I was admitted into the house of the Jesuits, to make a retreat under Father Villefort's direction; and he fed and gladdened my soul with the most delightful and soothing utterances of the Divine Word. That man of God can hardly be called a man; he is rather all heart, —a personification of heavenly charity. But no sooner were my eyes opened, than I saw around me many, many men of similar stamp, of whose existence the world knows nothing. What gentle kindness, what delicacy, what gracefulness, have I found in my intercourse with these Christians indeed! During my retreat, the venerable superior of the Jesuits visited me every evening, and poured the fragrant balm of heaven into my soul. He spoke to me but a few words; but they were words which expanded and grew as I listened to them, and filled me with joy and light and life.

That priest, so humble, and yet so powerful, had no need to speak to me; it was enough to see him: the remembrance of his features is even now enough to place me in the presence of God, and to make my whole soul glow with living gratitude. I cannot find words to express all my gratitude; I should need a thousand tongues to tell the love I feel for these men of God,—for M. Theodore de Bussières, that minister and forerunner of Mary—for the family of the Laferronnays, whom I regard with a veneration and an affection above all words.

At length the 31st of January dawned upon me, and I found myself surrounded with an atmosphere of tenderness and sympathy. How gladly would I know each one of those pious souls, that I might express my fervent gratitude! May they all ever pray for me, even as I pray for them!

O Rome, what grace and blessing have I found in thy sacred bosom! The Mother of my Lord and Saviour had arranged all that concerned me; she had brought a French priest to address me in my mother-tongue at the solemn moment of my baptism,—I mean M. Dupanloup, whose memory is linked indissolubly to that of the most profound emotions of my life. Happy they whose privilege it was to listen to him; for the echoes of that mighty address which the press has repeated can give no idea of what it really was. I felt that he too was inspired by her of whom he was speaking.

I will not relate the circumstances of my baptism, my confirmation, and my first communion,—suffice it to say, that I received all these ineffable graces in that one day at the hands of his Eminence Cardinal Patrizi vicar of his Holiness.

I should weary you, were I to attempt to tell you of all my impressions,—of all that I have seen and heard and felt. . . . if I were to make mention of the brotherly charity which has been so profusely lavished on me. I will mention only the very distinguished Cardinal Mezzofanti ; . . . . the Lord has endowed this illustrious person with the gift of tongues, in reward of a heart which makes itself every thing to every one.

One last great consolation was in reserve for me. You remember how earnestly I wished to see the Holy Father; indeed this desire, or this curiosity, had kept me at Rome longer than I intended. Little did I imagine under what circumstances my wish was to be gratified. It was as a new-born child of the Church that I was presented to the Father of all the faithful. From the moment of my baptism I had felt for the Sovereign Pontiff the reverent love of a son ; and I was delighted when it was told me that I was to be introduced into his presence by the reverend General of the Jesuits. Yet I trembled at the anticipation, for I had never mingled with great people; and the earth's greatest men sunk into insignificance in presence of this true greatness. I confess that all the royalties of earth seemed to me concentrated upon the head of him who wields on earth the powers of the world to come; upon that pontiff who succeeds in an unbroken line, to the keys of St. Peter, and to the high-priesthood of Aaron,—that representative of Jesus Christ himself, whose unshaken throne he fills.

Never shall I forget my awe and the beatings of my heart as I entered the Vatican, and passed through the vast courts, the imposing halls, which led to the sanctuary of the Pontiff. But all my anxiety was dispelled, to make room for surprise and wonder, when I saw him himself, so simple, so humble, so paternal. He was not a monarch, but a father, whose extreme kindness treated me as a beloved son.

My God! and will it be thus at that last day, when I shall appear before Thee, to give account of all the graces I have received? We tremble at thought of the majesty of God, and we fear His justice; but when His mercy shall be made known, our hopes and trust will revive, and with them a love and a gratitude without bounds.

Gratitude? yes, gratitude is henceforward

my law and my life. Never can I adequately express it in words; but I will endeavour to condense and suggest it by my actions.

The letters I have received from my family set me free from every engagement; and I offer my liberty to God, for all my life, to be employed in the service of the Church and of my brethren, under the protection of Mary. . . .

THE LATTER YEARS

OF

M. LE COMTE DE LAFERRONNAYS.

We feel it a duty to append to the narrative of this wonderful conversion two letters written to the *Union Catholique*, containing a brief account of the latter years of the Count de Laferronnays, whose name is so closely connected with that of M. Ratisbonne.

Rome, 19th January, 1842.

As you go along the Via Sacra, amongst the monuments which surround the ancient Forum with their picturesque ruins, you will notice that the temple of the twin-founders of Rome has suffered less than the rest from the ravages of time, and of the barbarian invaders of Rome. Christianity consecrated it, and so preserved its ruins. It was restored by a Pope in the sixth century; and became a church under the invocation of St. Cosmas and St. Damian—two brothers also, two Christian brothers, united during life by their mutual love, in death by martyrdom, in eternity by a common glory.

I love this church, as a monument of the earlier triumphs of the faith over paganism. Yesterday the Blessed Sacrament was exposed in it, and I went to visit it. My mind was full of the memory of M. de Laferronnays; and I was thinking that, but a year ago, he was kneeling near me in that church, praying at the tomb of the two martyrs, in presence of the Blessed Sacrament. I pictured him to myself as I had seen him, kneeling at the balustrade of the sanctuary, in an attitude of deep recollection, with his hands clasped, and his features composed into an angelic fervour. I read over again, with deep feeling, a prayer of reparation composed by him and written with his own hand, which he had let fall from his book as he was going away...... His death allows me to publish this touching prayer; and I think you will be glad to see some extracts from it. Surely it is for the glory of God; and it reveals to us the grandeur of his own soul and the fervour of his true repentance:

"O mysterious provision of a love surpassing knowledge, it is to Thee I owe my rescue from despair; Thou alone couldst, and Thou didst raise my soul out of the deadly despondency into which it was cast by the appalling and ever-present memory of my numberless and heinous sins...... I may show myself to the world as a living proof of Thine inexhaustible and most tender pity. I confess that, during the frightful madness to which I willingly abandoned myself for so many years, I have exceeded the extremest limits of ingratitude. From my childhood Thou hadst made me feel Thy protection, in placing me under the shield and direction of the tenderest and most pious of mothers, until the age when I was first called and admitted to Thy holy table. And still later, when my passions began to lay on me their degrading yoke, Thou, O my God, didst not cease to call me to Thyself. Often, amidst my wanderings, Thy voice reached my heart's depth in spite of all my resistance, and there uttered its severe counsels, its salutary threatenings; but, alas, Thy paternal admonitions did not lead me to repentance; they occasioned only transitory uneasiness, which I shook off by plunging yet deeper into sin. Later still, when Thou didst allow my lot to be united to that of the most excellent of women, Thou didst surround me with patterns and guides, who all pointed out to me the way of return unto Thee by walking in it themselves so faithfully. It is Thou, O God of goodness, who hast constantly and strangely preserved me during all the vicissitudes of my public life! In those days of revolution and wild folly, my sullied soul could have appeared before the tribunal of Thy justice only to hear the sentence of its everlasting condemnation. Thou didst allow death to threaten, but not to strike, my guilty head;

Thou didst wait still for my love! And these are but the least of the graces Thou hast bestowed on me; and how have I recompensed them!..... For more than half a century I have wilfully closed my eyes, that I might not see, and stopped my ears, that I might not hear. I sacrificed to the devil my rest, my life, my conscience, my soul, my salvation. Regardless of thy goodness, O my God, and putting away the Hand that was stretched out to save me, I took pleasure in accumulating sin upon sin, outrage upon outrage, as though I were eagerly bent on my own destruction. My iniquities towered like a great mountain up to the throne of Thy justice, and braved and provoked Thy vengeance...... O my God, never, never was any child of Thine so ungrateful, so guilty as I then was in Thy sight. And when at length, sated and palled with the poisoned pleasures of the world, exhausted by weariness and disgust, the snows of old age brought their warnings of death,—when serious thoughts and an awakening sorrow shook my soul,—then, horrified at myself, I thought my hour of forgiveness was past, that my tardy and insufficient remorse could no more disarm Thine anger: and I added to all my other sins this greatest sin—I doubted Thy mercy. But Thou didst send to my aid a guide, a comforter, who sustained my courage, and led me to Thy feet, and taught me to know Thee better, to implore Thy forgiveness and to hope."

Do not these pages, marked as they are by the tears of M. de Laferronnays, seem as though they were taken from that book in which St. Augustine, touched by God's grace, has treasured up the confession of his long wanderings, and the bitter expression of his regrets?

In one of his letters he gives an account of his conversion. We give it in his own words; for who would presume to substitute a narrative for these touching effusions of a penitent soul at the foot of the cross?

"The reflections I have had time enough to make during my long and lonely journey, have at length borne some fruit. When I reached Paris, I was convinced, and my mind was made up; my decision and my conviction are not the result of enthusiasm or of precipitation. Nor is it the brilliance of any light that might dazzle me that has opened my eyes: my soul has not been compelled to put itself on the defensive against the charm of a persuasive eloquence; whatever living convictions I have ever had spring from within me. I have yielded only after long and earnest resistance; the old man has struggled vigorously—the conflict has been long and desperate. But as I retraced my eight-and-fifty years, and examined calmly the long succession of days which were employed in sin; as I thought of the evil example I had given to others, and the scandal of which I have so often been the occasion; as I reflected that amongst this countless multitude of actions there was not one that was good,—I was horrified at myself, and conceived such a detestation of myself, that despair had well-nigh seized my heart, to the exclusion of true repentance. I passed several days of my journey in a state of violent and painful emotion. Then, all on a sudden, I know not how or why, I felt myself calm and almost happy, as though some gentle and soothing influence had sunk down into my soul. It was hope. I remembered that hope was not only permitted, but commanded as a duty, and that forgiveness was promised to the penitent sinner. I blessed and praised God for having awakened my conscience, and for soothing my remorse by hope and faith. And in this state of mind I reached Paris. I felt now that I have no more to dread human respect, no more false shame to overcome. One of my first visits was paid to your friend in the Rue de Grenelle, to whom I gave your letter. I had a long interview with him. I was anxious that *the man* should know *the man* before *the judge* heard the tale of *the culprit*. I told him all the story of my sinful life; and I assure you I did it sincerely, and without any conscious desire to exculpate myself. I felt a kind of comfort and of ease in thus giving him my confidence, even without imposing on him any obligation of secrecy; it seemed to me a fitting and useful penance. After these confessions made to the man, it was neither painful nor difficult to me to repeat them at the feet of the judge who has received the noble mission, the consoling power, to pardon and to absolve. My habitual vanity made a faint resistance, but a better feeling vanquished it; and I have a good hope that God, who reads all hearts, saw my sincere repentance, and that His infinite mercy has ratified the sentence of His minister. And now ten days have passed. I feel with delight and with gratitude that my resolutions are stronger day by day. My reason, subjugated by grace, humbly accepts the teaching of faith; my understanding no longer loses itself in vain and fruitless analyses of mysteries beyond its range; I believe in all simplicity, and I find it a blessing and a boon to be able to believe that which commands nothing but what is good, and promises nothing but happiness."

This was a great and solemn crisis in the life of Count de Laferronnays. Having once resolved, he never wavered, but steadily persevered. Nothing could throw him back, or quell his courage. He *believed*, and from that moment his whole life was raised up to the high level of his faith. The terrors of human respect, which are generally so mighty in public men, never shook his noble heart. It was so high a blessedness, so great an honour, as he said, to possess the Catholic faith, that he could not but walk manfully erect in its divine light. While he was as humble and simple as a child in all his practices of devotion, his soul grasped and held with a generous fervour the loftiest inspirations of Christianity. He felt and realised all its strong resolves, all its tender yet energetic emotions, its meek compassion, its sublime self-devotedness, its high thoughts, its far-reaching views, its rarest and choicest suggestions. Certainly his was a grand and a noble soul; and religion, in pervading him with its mighty life, had still further raised and ennobled him.

I do not affect, however, to pronounce his eulogy; I wish you simply to see him as he really was. Here is an extract from a letter written in reference to a friend who had lost his only child, a tenderly-beloved daughter:

"What a wretched return home! What a moment was their arrival at L——*without her!* What a void around them, within them; and what a despoiled and desolate life is theirs! All these thoughts oppress the heart and weary the mind, and lay him who has the blessedness of believing prostrate at the foot of the cross. What can we ask or expect of man in these great crises of the soul?

How can the most quick and tender sympathy reach a grief so poignant? No, my dear friend, the deepest affection is powerless here; it can find no words to heal a wound like this. Religion alone, and unfailingly, suggests the words which the smitten heart craves to hear; it alone has the right and the power to take from our tears their excess of bitterness; it alone dares speak of hope in presence of despair; it alone can tell of a compensating future to those who have no longer either past or present. Religion alone has the sublime power to raise from the dust the stricken soul, by speaking of the certainty of the eternal reunion of those whom death's fell stroke has for awhile sundered. O, how I pity those who suffer, and yet are so miserable as to feel any doubt on these grand and comforting truths! Whenever a fresh grief assails the heart, how sad not to know where to look for succour; to be obliged to wrestle with anguish and with despair *alone*. The soul of the Christian, on the contrary, fit is ever a sure refuge at the foot of the cross; there it pours forth its tears, and the wail of its grief: thence it draws the strength and the courage of resignation, which is simply impossible without the faith which gives hope...."

The same grace which had led him to the true source of consolation, revealed to him also the value and worth in the eyes of God of those souls which sin has degraded, and which the Christian faith can restore, while the world crushes them with its scorn. What striking words are these, in reference to a distinguished person, who was drawing near to the close of a life of most shameful disorder:

"That head once so high, so insolent,—now bowed down to the grave; that countenance, so witty, so merry, so boldly bad in its expression,—now so gloomy, so besotted, and all its fire extinguished! All this slow and humiliating decomposition of a form and a constitution which was the matter of so much pride, the instrument and incentive of such daring abuses! What lessons are these! Well, my friend, this decrepitude, this moral death, this loathsome close of a scandalous life disgusts the world; it flees in horror, or contempt, or pity. But God is there still. He judges not as men judge; with one word, with one look, He can raise again that degraded soul, and renew and sanctify it. And he, whom we look upon with so much disdain, with a pity so insulting—could he but once raise his heart and his eyes to heaven—this man, so worn out by sin, has perhaps his prepared place on high! Yet a few days of suffering and of humiliation, and it may be he will look down on us with pity and compassion! Our sublime religion teaches us thus much; and these people, forsooth, tell you that it is mere foolery! They kill you, they wither and waste you, and then give you up to annihilation; and they call **this** *philosophy*, the love of wisdom!"

The ambition of M. de Laferronnays had never been tempted by the glitter of greatness, nor by the desire of playing an important part in those councils on which hung suspended the destiny of France and of all Europe. He wrote thus, on the very day of his nomination to the Ministry of Foreign Affairs:

"My friend, I am very wretched and very unfortunate. In spite of all my resolutions, I have accepted this dreaded office. I might, perhaps, have resisted the wishes of the king; but I have yielded to his sadness, to his goodness; and here I am, chained to the oar. You will read my sentence this morning in the *Moniteur;* and you will be able to say to yourself that, even in my new position, coveted as it is by so many, France does not contain a more pitiable and unfortunate creature than I am. It is a singular thing, this destiny,—and I can make nothing of mine; for it drives me always in the direction I am anxious to avoid. But it has never behaved so badly, never played me such a trick as this. If ever you happen to hear that I am ambitious, that I love what men call honours, and the whirl and bustle of business, and the importance of a great place, or any of those great human absurdities in virtue of which men worry one another, and overturn empires, pray make haste and tell them it is all false."

But it was from a graver and loftier point of view that he looked down upon these *human absurdities* after his conversion. He was raised above them by all the height of that eternity which was his habitual thought.

"When it is at the close of fifty years of life that these grand thoughts of death and its results lay hold on one, do you think it well to try to distract one's mind, and that one is wrong in not feeling disposed to make the attempt? Will you deem me very absurd in desiring that nothing may ever lessen the influence of these thoughts upon me,—thoughts which are most mighty and influential in silence and in solitude? No, my friend, I am very sure that you understand me; and that if any imperious duty compelled me to give it my feeble remnant of strength, you would be able to pity me, and to appreciate the immense sacrifice which it would be to me at my age, and with such a terrible past. Every moment is of infinite value; one fears every thing that might divert or alter the employment of these precious moments. I have lost so much time, that every thing which stops me on my way, or throws me back, may expose me to the risk of being surprised before I reach my goal. Perhaps I am too singular in all this; the politicians of your *salons*, and your editors of journals, don't think of these things; and in urging me as they do, they care very little where I should fall at the last. But it is of great importance to me. And so they may rest assured that, unless I feel convinced that it is the will of God concerning me, no considerations will induce me to yield."

Most of the admirable letters were written from Rome. It was at Rome, that pure source of the faith, that this noble soul had drunk in the copious dews of heaven, and struck its roots so deep in so short a time; it was in the genial warmth of that Catholic atmosphere that it had opened its loveliest flowers, and diffused its most fragrant perfumes. And it was on that hallowed soil, which he had found so propitious to him, that the venerable tree fell, almost pressed to earth by the weight of its fruit,—its tender charity, its sincere and unaffected piety, its lowly repentance, and all the other graces of which his vigorous old age, renewed by faith, had been so fruitful. And the sweet odour of his sanctity abides in the Church of Rome, as an added glory and adornment; in the memory of all his friends, as a powerful charm which binds them or draws them to Christianity; and in the very hearts he has bruised so sore, as a balm of heaven to their wounds, as a manifest pledge of eternal life.

SECOND LETTER.

Rome, 29th January, 1842.

I had gathered the details enclosed herewith a few days after the death of M. de Laferronnays. By some unhappy inadvertence, the letter, which I thought was on its way to you, was left in my desk. I still forward it, notwithstanding the delay which I deplore; the memory of M. de Laferronnays cannot be so soon effaced in France, even in these lively times when an event can scarcely preserve a past of twenty-four hours. . . . .

Alas, alas, another grievous loss, a loss quite unexpected too! The day before yesterday, at this very hour, my old and dear friend, Count de Laferronnays, was with me to introduce a young painter whose genius and piety had inspired him with a lively interest. When I reproached him for being late, he said: "I could not come sooner; I had an important letter to write, and it was indispensable that it should go off to-day. . . . " He little thought, nor did I, how indispensable it was that he should avail himself of that courier. I left him to pay some visits, without bidding him adieu even; and I was never to see him again alive. . . . . He accompanied my children, who were going out with his daughter, and his son-in law, the Count de Meun; they went together to St. John

Lateran, where he prayed for a considerable time before the Blessed Sacrament, as was his wont. He complained a little of a pain in the chest, which came on at intervals, and was so sharp and sudden that it prevented his walking; but in all other respects he was as cheerful and lively as usual. My children met him again at Benediction, in the chapel at the Perpetual Adoration, on the Quirinal.

There was on that evening a brilliant *fête* at the Austrian Embassy. Madame de Laferronnays was to take her daughters there; and while they were dressing, M. de Laferronnays amused himself by playing with his grandchild. It was between half-past eight and nine; he complained still of his pain; but as it was habitual, they were sorry for it, but felt no serious anxiety. They attributed it to the effect of a *brasero* they had put into the room to warm it, and the excessive heat of which had drawn the blood to his chest. But, however that may have been, they sent for the physician. Madame de Laferronnays wrote a few words to the Abbé Gerbet; but his state occasioned so little alarm, that M. de Menn expressed to his sister-in-law his regret at Madame de Laferronnays' tendency to exaggerate her husband's ailments. The letter to the Abbé Gerbet was not sent immediately. When the physician arrived, he advised bleeding, and a surgeon was sent for. But the pain became easier; they thought the crisis past, and stopped the bleeding. However, the return of the pain made them send again for the surgeon, who made two fruitless attempts to bleed him again. He now suffered most acutely, and cries of anguish escaped him in spite of his self-control. During this time, his wife —his angelic wife—was in a state of keen distress; going and coming, trying to avoid hearing his moans; when a few words disclosed to her the imminence of the danger. She sat down by the bed on which he had just been laid, took his hand in hers, and did not leave him again. She sat in perfect calmness, full of gentleness and resignation. Meanwhile the Abbé Gerbet arrived, approached the bed, and gave him his blessing; and then, at some questions addressed to him, the beloved patient replied with a surprising burst of fervour: " Yes, yes; oh, yes, I do repent of all my sins. Oh, yes, I do love God with all my soul!" And taking the crucifix, he pressed it eagerly to his lips, and repeated several times this simple invocation: "My God, have mercy on me! Holy Virgin, pray for me; come to my aid!" He had enjoyed the privilege of communicating the day before. In this extreme danger his confessor gave him absolution; he received it with profound repentance, and his eyes were blinded with tears of sorrow and of gratitude. Then his face regained its usual serenity, and betokened the calmness, the divine peace, the heavenly joy of his soul.

"How happy I feel now!" said he, with failing voice, but with a smile of absolute confidence and hope; "how happy I feel now!" But soon his breathing became more difficult: "Adieu," said he to his beloved wife, taking her hand in his, "adieu, my dear children!"... and in a few moments his soul, so pure, so noble, so truly Christian, appeared before God; while his young daughters were kneeling beside his bed in their gay festival dresses.

It was a heart-rending scene. It was now only half-past ten o'clock. What an unexpected bereavement! what a thunder-stroke! But this sudden death, which snapped in two hours bonds so strong and so sweet, came not unlooked-for by him whom it smote. For many years he had been awaiting his summons, and prepared himself every day for death, as though each day were certainly his last. On that very day he had said to his wife, on his return home: "I have been to Sta. Maria Maggiore. I knelt down, and implored the Madonna; and I said to God: Behold me, O Lord, I am ready: take me if Thou willest to have me; but if Thou permittest me to remain yet longer on earth, my life shall be consecrated to thy glory alone!" The thought of death had become habitual to him, yet it did not ruffle the deep calmness of his heart, or affect the simple gentle gaiety of his conversation; a profound distaste for pleasures and honours had detached him from those illusions of which he had felt all the nothingness, and the energy of his faith disclosed to him, beyond the grave, the only hopes which could fill and content his magnificent soul. Rome, with the solemn associations of its ruins, deepened the tone of those grave and holy thoughts which were most congenial to him. I have before me a letter which he wrote nearly a year ago; a few extracts from it will reveal to you his habitual state of mind:

"I leave Rome with regret; and but for the important matters which summon me to France, I should certainly have prolonged my stay. I suppose it is because I see it now with other eyes, and feel more deeply all its significance. For him who is blessed with faith, for him who has ever held lonely converse with himself in that city of silence and of faith, Rome is the city to live and to die in. I admire as much as any one these colossal ruins, which give one so grand an idea of what ancient Rome must have been, and of the wonderful people who raised them. I can well understand why the imagination should be at once enthralled and excited amidst these stately relics; yet it is not the ruins which fascinate me, nor the recollections of olden time which make me sorry to leave it. It is the soil of those theatres moistened with the blood of thousands of martyrs, the precious remains of those heroes of the faith, which are here preserved and venerated on the very spot of their glorious agony; it is the sacred dust of the catacombs, that hallowed ground which has witnessed the sufferings and the triumphs of the Church, its tribulations and its glories; it is that unshaken rock, against which the impotent efforts of impiety, heresy, and philosophism, have been broken and thrown back, age after age,—this throne of the poor fisherman, set up on the ruins of the throne of the Cæsars, the rulers of the world! And all that is here, all around me as I walk. O my friend, how can one see all this, and not believe? how can one help feeling at Rome some presentiment of our eternal destiny? how can we miss seeing whence our souls came, and whither they are going? How can people come to Rome only to see lifeless stones? Above all, how can they have the heart, when surrounded by so many witnesses of God and of His power, of the Catholic religion and its truth,—how can they stoop to petty criticisms of incidental abuses, of the political state of the country, or of the peculiarity of certain religious usages and ceremonies—ceremonies and usages of which our little minds know neither the meaning nor the necessity? To a Catholic soul Rome is simply Catholic Rome; it is the land of Catholic memorials, of Catholic miracles, of Catholic hopes. Here one's faith grows stronger; here the Catholic raises a corner of that veil which shrouds the sublime mysteries of our religion; here the heart of the Catholic sees with a clear and distinct intuition the vanity and nothingness of the pomps and glories of this world, and already breathes the calm and genial atmosphere of the unvarying eternity. I saw Rome three times while my heart was yet frozen in religious indifference; and being neither an artist nor a poet, I was terribly tired,—just as one grows tired of a long harangue in an unknown tongue. But now I have the faculty which enables me to see, to hear, to understand, to feel. My days are all too short, I am so eager to see and to know every thing. My soul is filled with most delightful emotions—emotions which are the more living and exquisite that they are so new and fresh to me. May God grant that I may once again see Rome.... Yes, it is at Rome I would fain live and die...."

And God heard his prayer. The Count de Laferronnays did return to Rome; he lived there amid all the aids and consolations of the faith, and he died amidst all its graces and benedictions.

His death occasioned many sorrows and many tears. He was so affectionate and so gentle, that he was loved by every one. *Cunctorum amans, cunctis amabilissimus.* His body was embalmed, and lay in state three days in the Palazzo Spina. Many prelates and priests of France made it a point to say Mass in that quiet chapel. The venerable Father de Geramb passed a whole night in prayer beside his bier—last and deepest expression of a friendship begun in youthful dissipation, sanctified afterwards by that religion which had made the one a pattern of true piety in the world, and the other a model of austerities and of penitence in a cloister of La Trappe. Every homage that could honor his memory and comfort his bereaved family was paid to his remains. His own numerous friends, many illustrious foreigners, the ambassadors of France, Austria, and Naples, and crowds of noble women, who prayed and mourned apart, formed the glorious procession of his funeral. The sorrow of all these sympathising souls was soothed by an extraordinary event connected with this sudden death. The day after, in that very church, and a few steps only from the bier prepared for his funeral, M. Alphonse Ratisbonne, for whose conversion he had breathed his latest prayers, was smitten down like St. Paul by a supernatural vision, and arose imploring holy baptism, and blessing the memory of the illustrious deceased, who had prayed for him without knowing him. Thus God Himself seemed to authorise us to believe the everlasting blessedness of the soul of our beloved friend; for while we were here on earth offering our tears, our prayers, and the precious blood of Jesus Christ for his repose, the power of his intercession in heaven was attested in our midst by a miracle!

THE END.

PUBLICATIONS OF P. J. KENEDY,

EXCELSIOR

Catholic Publishing House,

5 BARCLAY ST., Near Broadway,

Opposite the Astor House,   NEW YORK.

All for the Sacred Heart of Jesus. Dedicated to associates of League of Sacred Heart. Net	.50
Adelmar the Templar, a Tale of the Crusades	.40
Adventures and Daring Deeds of Michael Dwyer	1.00
All about Knock. Complete account of Cures, etc	1.00
Apparitions and Miracles at Knock, paper cover	.25
Atala. By Chateaubriand. Doré's Illustrations, 4to gilt	3.00
Battle of Ventry Harbor, paper cover	.20
Bible, Douay. Octavo, large print. Vellum cloth	2.50
The same, American Morocco, gilt edges	5.00
The same, Turkey Morocco, antique, gilt edges	10.00
Bible, Haydock's, Style G. Fr. Morocco paneled, 2 clasps	18.00
The same, Style H., Turkey Morocco beveled	25.00
Blanche, or the great evils of Pride	.40
Blind Agnese, Little Spouse of the Blessed Sacrament	.60
British Catholic Poets, red line, gilt edges	1.25
Brooks (Senator) and Hughes (Archbishop) Controversy	.75
Burke's Lectures and Sermons 1st series, cloth	2.00
The same, full gilt side and edges	3.00
Burke's Lectures and Sermons, 2d series cloth	2.00
The same, full gilt side and edges	3.00
Burke's Lectures and Sermons in Ireland, cloth	2.50
The same, full gilt side and edges	3.00
Burke's Lectures—The set complete, 3 vols, plain	6.00
The same gilt	9.00
Burke's Reply to Froude, Ireland's case stated	1.00
Cannon's Poems and Dramas. Red line, gilt edges	1.25

Catholic Prayer-Books, 25c., 50c., up to **12 00**

☞ Any of above books sent free by mail on receipt of price. Agents wanted everywhere to sell above books, to whom liberal terms will be given. Address

P. J. KENEDY, Excelsior Catholic Publishing House, 5 Barclay Street, New York.

Publications of P. J. Kenedy, 5 Barclay St. N. Y.

Canon Schmid's Exquisite Tales, 6 vols, Illustrated...	3.00
Cannon's Practical Spelling Book	.25
Captain of the Club, a Story for Boys	.75
Carroll O'Donoghue. By Christine Faber	1.25
Carpenter's Speller and Definer	.25
Catechism Third Plenary Council, large, No. 2, paper, per 100 net	4.50
The same, abridged No. 1, paper per 100 net	3.50
The same, No. 2, cloth flexible, per 100 net	6.00
The same, No 1, " " " " "	3.50
Catechism, General, National Council, paper per 100 net	2.00
The same, abridged paper cover, per 100 net	1.50
Catechism, Butler's large, paper per 100 net	2.50
The same, abridged, paper per 100 net	1.50
The same, cloth, Illustrated Mass Prayers	.30
Catechism, The, or Short abridgment, New York, per 100 net	2.00
Catechism, Boston. Prayers at Mass, etc., paper per 100 net	2.00
Catechism, Keenan's Doctrinal, cloth	.50
Catechism, Poor Man's, large and thick.	.40
Catechism, Spanish, Ripalda, paper cover	.12
Catechism, Spanish, Astete, paper cover	.15
Catechism, Spanish, Nuevo Caton, paper cover	.15
Catholic Christian Instructed, paper .20, cloth	.30
Catholic Excelsior Library, 6 vols, per set	4.50
Catholic Faith and Morals, By L'Homond	1.00
Catholic Fireside Library, 10 vols, per set	7.50
Catholic Flowers from Protestant Gardens, gilt	1.25
Catholic Home Library, 8 vols, per set	4.00
Catholic Juvenile Library, 6 vols, per set	2.40
Catholic Keepsake Library, 6 vols, per set	4.50
Catholic Missions and Missionaries. By Shea	2.50
Catholic Offering or Gift Book. By Abp. Walsh	1.00
Catholic Piety, (Prayer Book). Prices range upwards from	.60
Catholic School Book	.25
Chambers' English Literature, 2 vols. Octavo	5.00

Catholic Prayer-Books, 25c., 50c., up to **12 00**

☞ Any of above books sent free by mail on receipt of price. Agents wanted everywhere to sell above books, to whom liberal terms will be given. Address

P. J. KENEDY, Excelsior Catholic Publishing House, 5 Barclay Street, New York.

Publications of P. J. Kenedy, 5 Barclay St. N. Y.

Chancellor and his Daughter. Sir Thos. More	1.25
Christian Etiquette. For Ladies and Gentlemen	1.25
Christian Maiden's Love. By Louis Veuillot	.75
Christian's Rule of Life. By St. Liguori	.50
Christian Virtues. By St. Liguori	1.00
Christopher Columbus. Illustrated, 4to gilt	3.00
Chivalrous Deed. By Christine Faber	1.25
Clifton Tracts Library of Controversy, 4 vols	3.00
Collins' Poem. Red line, gilt edge	1.25
Converted Jew. M. A. Ratisbonne	.50
Countess of Glosswood	.75
Crown of Jesus (Prayer Book). Prices range upwards from	1.00
Daily Companion (Prayer Book). Prices upwards from	.25
Daily Piety, (Prayer Book). Prices upwards from	.20
Dalaradia. By William Collins	.75
Davis' Poems and Essays, complete	1.50
Devout Manual, 18mo, (Prayer Book). Prices upwards from	.75
Devout Manual, 32mo, (Prayer Book). Prices upwards from	.25
Dick Massey, a Story of Irish Evictions	1.00
Diploma of Children of Mary Society, per 100 net	3.00
Doctrinal Catechism. By Rev. Stephen Keenan	.50
Dove of the Tabernacle. By Rev. T. H. Kinane	.75
Drops of Honey. By Father Zelus Animarum	.75
Drops of Honey Library—9 volumes, per set	6.75
Elevation of the soul to God	.75
Empire and Papacy. The Money God	1.25
Epistles and Gospels, 24mo. Good Type	.20
Erin go Bragh, Songster. Paper cover	.25
Evenings at School. New edition Net	1.00
Exercises of the Way of the Cross, paper cover	.05
Faber's (Christine) Works, 4 vols, large, 12mo. per set	5.00
Fair France during the Second Empire	1.00
Fair Maid of Connaught. By Mrs. Hughes	.75
Faugh a Ballagh Songster. Paper cover	.25
Feasts and Fasts. By Rev. Alban Butler	1.25

Catholic Prayer-Books, 25c., 50c., up to **12 00**

☞ Any of above books sent free by mail on receipt of price. Agents wanted everywhere to sell above books, to whom liberal terms will be given. Address

P. J. KENEDY, Excelsior Catholic Publishing House, 5 Barclay Street, New York.

Publications of P. J. Kenedy, 5 Barclay St. N. Y.

Feast of Flowers and The Stoneleighs	.75
Fifty Reasons why the R. C. Religion, etc.	.25
Flowers of Piety (Prayer Book). Prices upwards from.	.85
Following of Christ. A Kempis, 1.25, 1.00 and	.40
Foster Sisters. By Agnes M. Stewart	1.25
From Error to Truth, or the Deacon's Daughters	.75
Furniss' Tracts for Spiritual Reading	1.00
Gems of Prayer, (Prayer Book). Prices upwards from.	.25
Glimpse of G' and other Poems. E. C. Kane	.50
Glories of Ma. St L. Liguori. Large, 12mo.	1.25
Golden Book of Confraternities	.50
Golden Hour Library, 6 vols, red edges. per set	3.00
Good Reading For Young Girls	.75
Gordon Lodge, or Retribution	1.25
Grace O'Halloran. By Agnes M. Stewart	.75
Green Shores of Erin. Drama, net	.25
Grounds of the Catholic Doctrine	.25
Guardian's Mystery. By Christine Faber	1.25
Handy Andy. By Lover. Large edition	1.25
Hay on Miracles. Explanation, etc.	1.00
History of the Catholic Church in the U. S. J. G. Shea.	2.00
History of Ireland. By Moore, 2 volumes	3.00
History of Modern Europe. By J. G. Shea	1.25
History of the United States. By Frost.	1.25
Hours with the Sacred Heart	.50
Irish Fireside Library, 6 vols, 16mo	6.00
Irish Fireside Stories, Tales and Legends	1.25
Irish National Songster. Comic and Sentimental	1.00
Irish Patriot's Library, 6 vols, 12mo.	7.50
Irish Race in the Past and Present	2.50
Irish Rebels in English Prisons	1.50
Irish Scholars of the Penal Days	1.00
Jesus in the Tabernacle. New Meditations	.50
Keenan's Doctrinal Catechism	.50
Keeper of the Lazaretto. By Souvestre	.40
Key of Heaven, 18mo, (Prayer Book). Large. Prices up from	.75

Catholic Prayer-Books, 25c., 50c., up to 12.00

☞ Any of above books sent free by mail on receipt of price. Agents wanted everywhere to sell above books, to whom liberal terms will be given. Address

P. J. KENEDY, Excelsior Catholic Publishing House, 5 Barclay Street, New York.

www.ingramcontent.com/pod-product-compliance
Lightning Source LLC
Chambersburg PA
CBHW030340170426
43202CB00010B/1189